So here goes

Edna

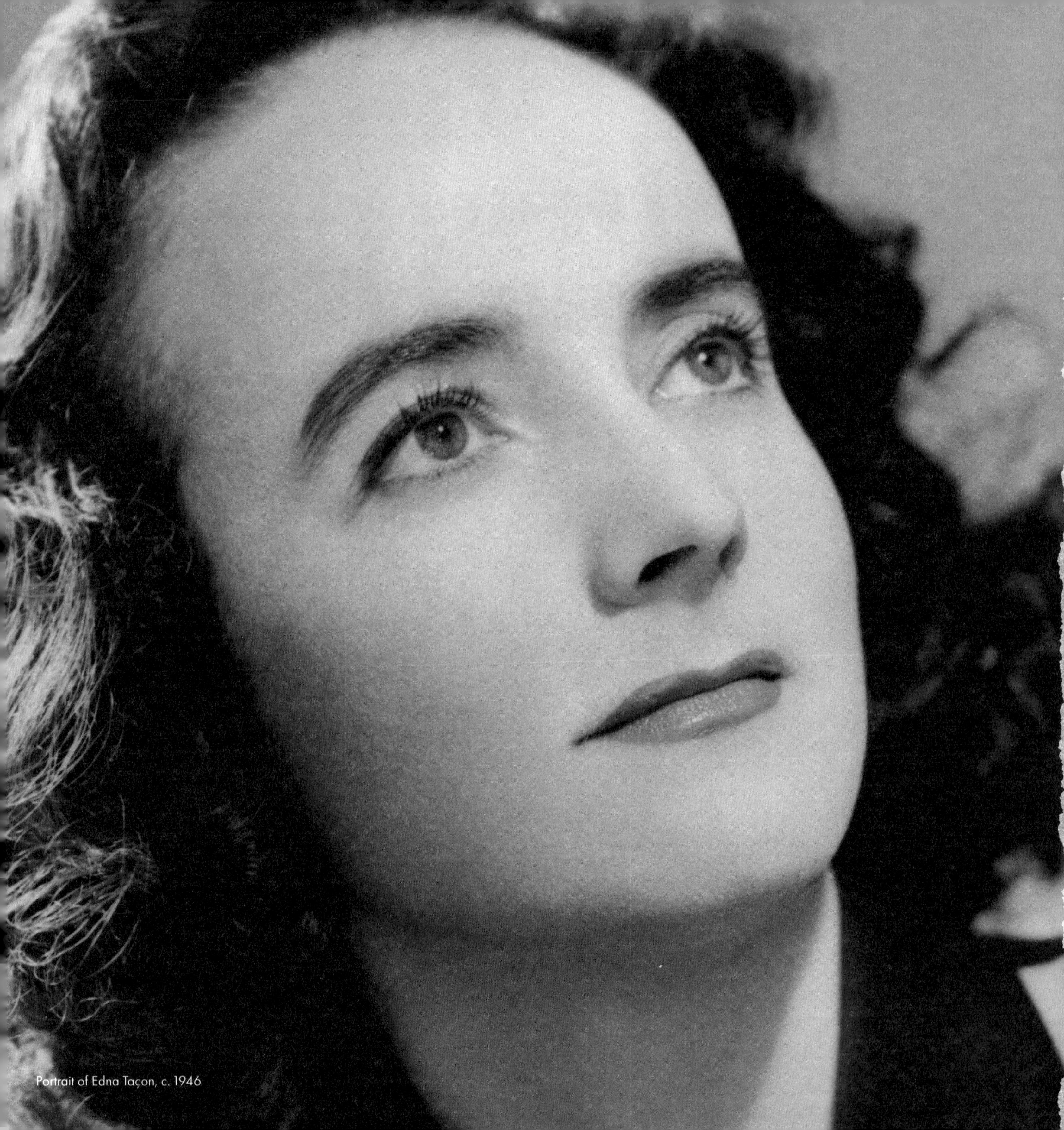

Portrait of Edna Taçon, c. 1946

Renée van der Avoird

EDNA TAÇON

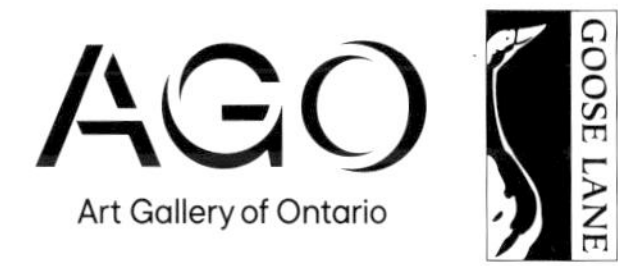

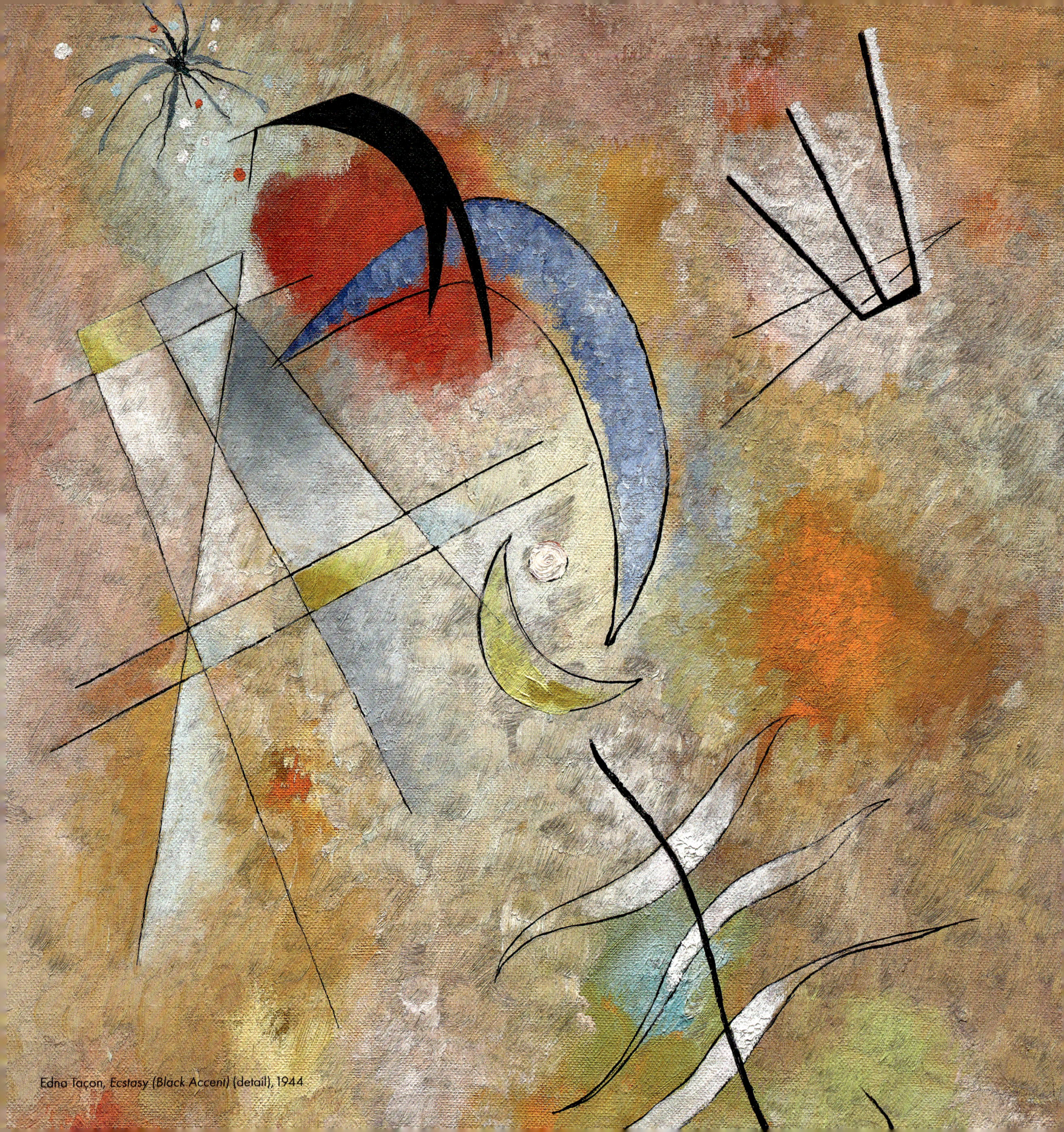

Edna Taçon, *Ecstasy (Black Accent)* (detail), 1944

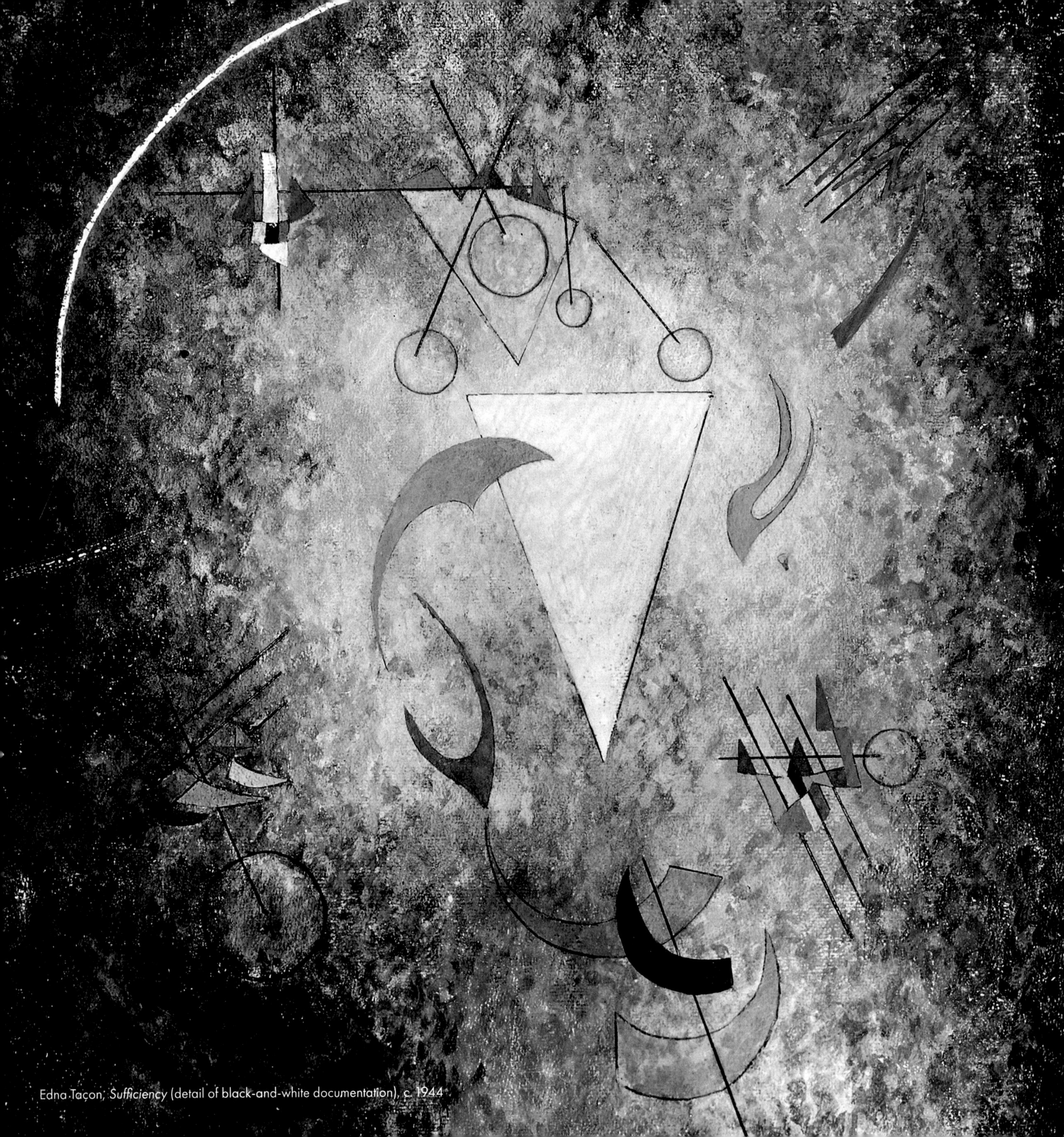

Edna Taçon, *Sufficiency* (detail of black-and-white documentation), c. 1944

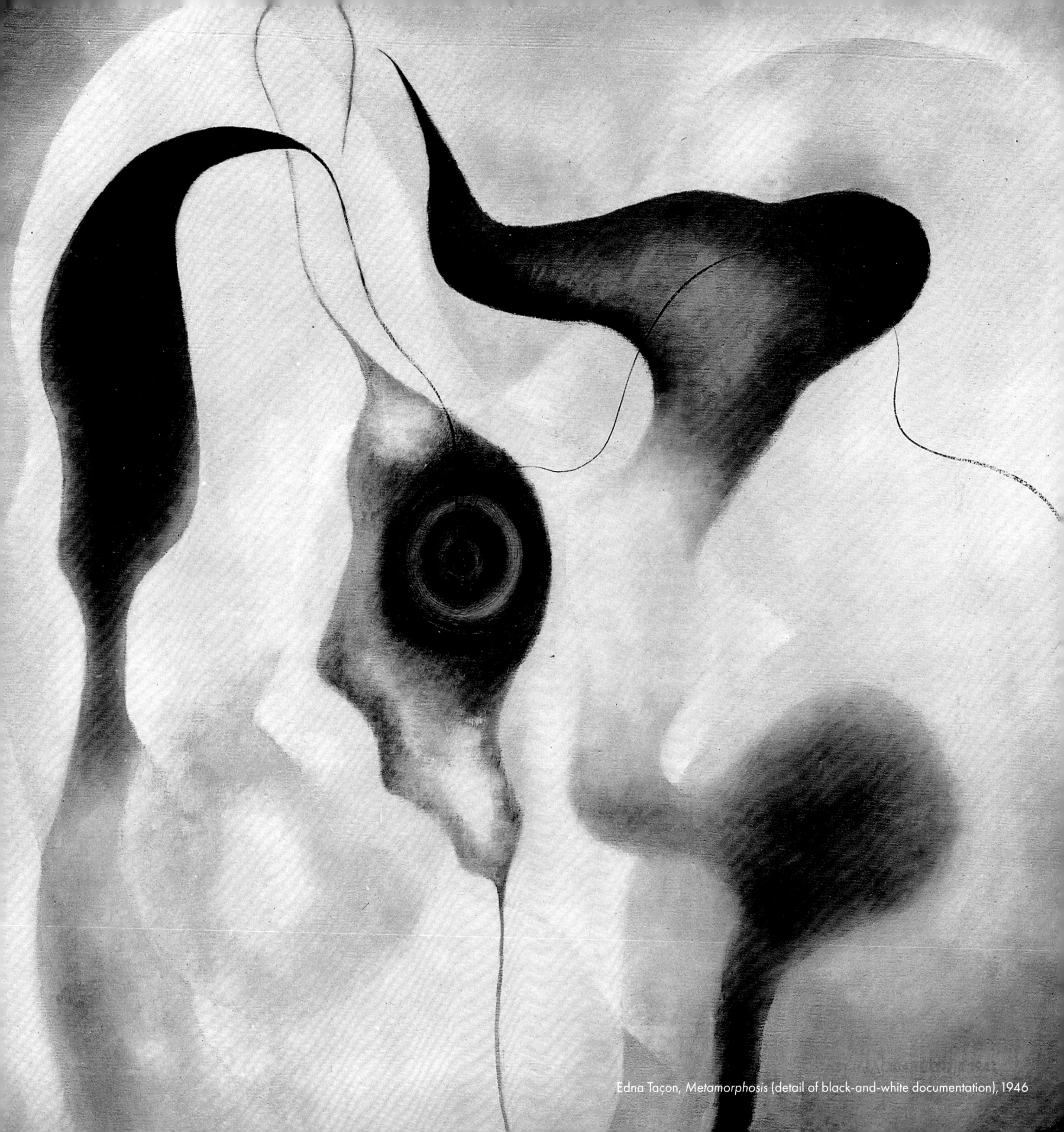

Edna Taçon, *Metamorphosis* (detail of black-and-white documentation), 1946

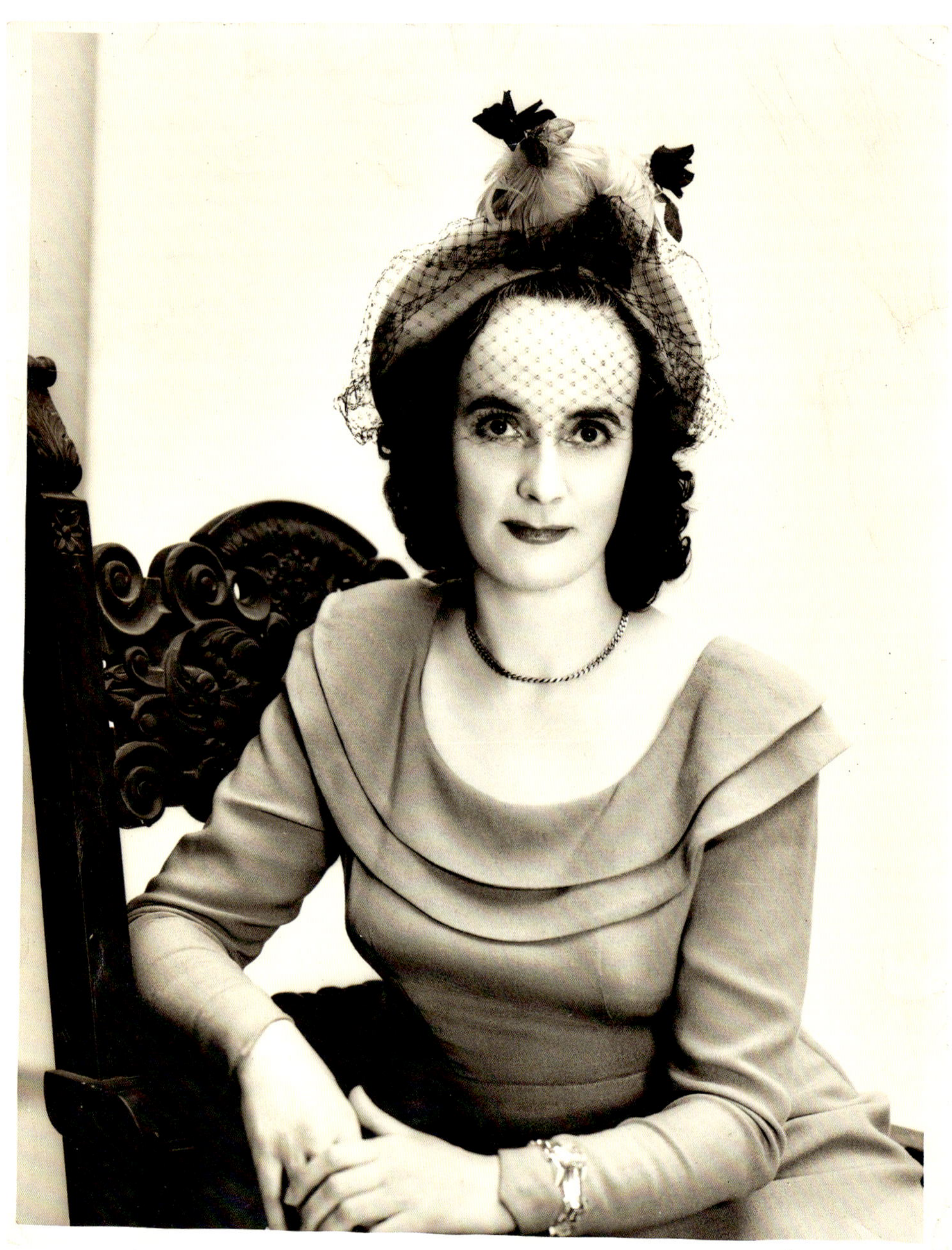

Edna Taçon wearing a hat, c. 1950s

Over the last century, history books have seldom mentioned the prolific painter Edna Taçon and her innumerable contributions to modernism. Born in Milwaukee, Wisconsin, in 1905 and raised in Goderich, Ontario, she became very active in the Canadian arts scene during the 1940s—specifically in Toronto, where she played a key role in the popularization of non-objective, abstract painting. Taçon split her time between Toronto and New York, going on to make significant connections at the Solomon R. Guggenheim Museum and work alongside leading avant-garde artists such as Lawren Harris and Hilla Rebay. Music was a highly instructive component of her practice, as were the teachings of Wassily Kandinsky, and she carved a unique path forward by intertwining her formal training as a violinist with her explorations into visual art. Her paintings and collages were deemed radical at the time, and she faced societal pressures as a woman commanding space in a male-dominated industry, in addition to living on the geographic periphery of two vastly different art landscapes. While Taçon succeeded professionally during her lifetime, she faded into relative art-historical obscurity following her death in 1980.

Curated by Renée van der Avoird in close consultation with the artist's family, *EDNA TAÇON* seeks to uncover her legacy for new generations and position her as an influential modern painter. Featuring a key selection of Taçon's rarely seen oil paintings, watercolours, and paper collages, the exhibition also illuminates aspects of her personal life through archival sketches, correspondence, and photographs of the artist. This publication is the first-ever monograph devoted to Taçon's œuvre and includes research that has been gleaned from newly uncovered archival sources and interviews with the artist's family members.

I would foremost like to acknowledge Renée van der Avoird, Associate Curator, Canadian Art, for the illuminating new scholarship she has contributed to Taçon's archive and for her leadership in championing the artist's work for many years. Additionally, thank you to Julian Cox, Deputy Director & Chief Curator; Nadia Abraham, Interpretive Planner; Kate Halpenny, Chief Development Officer, and her team for their fundraising efforts; the Creative Studio for developing various exhibition graphics; and the Publishing team for producing this exemplary publication.

We extend our sincere gratitude to the entire Taçon family for sharing their time, emotional labour, and incredible insights, in addition to loaning a great number of works for this exhibition. Thank you in particular to Paul & Susan Taçon for their support of this publication as well. Additionally, we thank Swee C. Goh in memory of Lilian Goh.

Taçon exhibited extensively in group shows during her lifetime, yet she did not experience the same critical attention and celebration as her male contemporaries. We are pleased to mount the most expansive presentation of her work to date and her first-ever solo exhibition at a major institution anywhere in the world. By reintroducing audiences to the remarkable and complex work of Edna Taçon, we hope that she will receive lasting recognition as the leading proponent of non-objective painting in Canada.

Stephan Jost
Michael & Sonja Koerner Director, and CEO

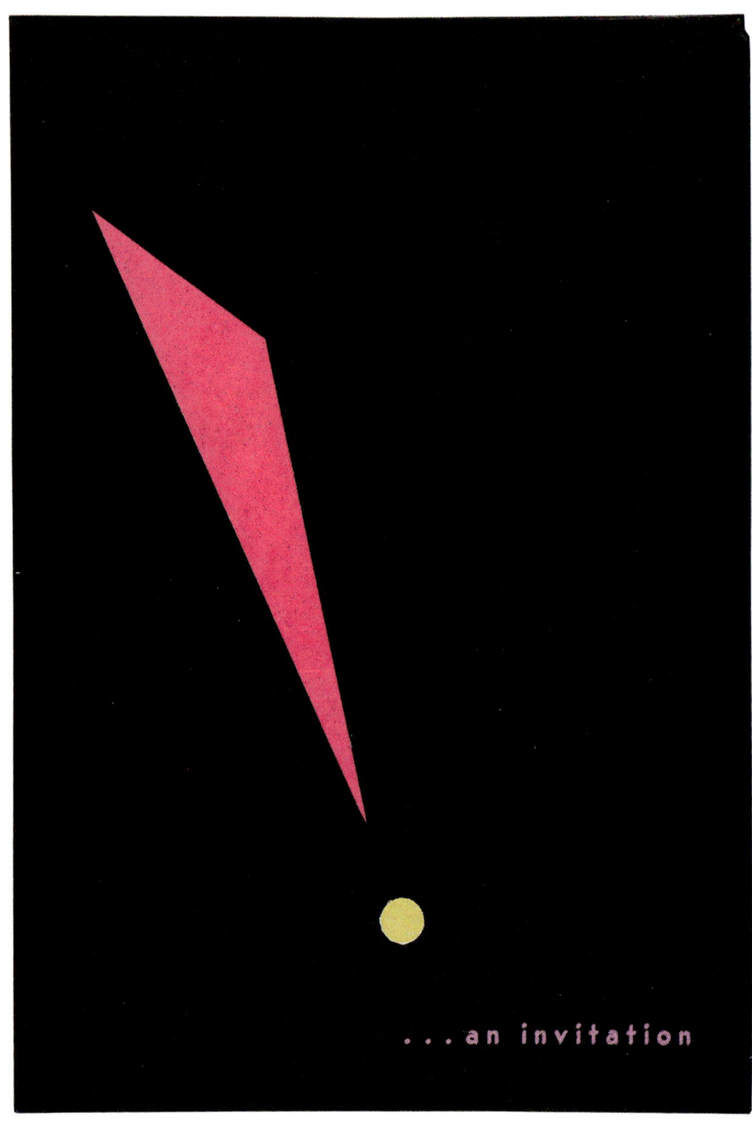

Exhibition pamphlet for *Non-Objective Pictures
(Paintings and Paper Plastics)* by Edna Taçon,
Studio 83, New York City, 1941

FERN GOLTRE

INVITES YOU TO AN EXHIBITION
OF
NON-OBJECTIVE PICTURES
(PAINTINGS AND PAPER PLASTICS)

by

EDNA TACON

AT

STUDIO 83

19 WEST THIRTY-FIRST STREET
NEW YORK CITY
TUESDAY, OCTOBER TWENTY-FIRST, 1941

R.S.V.P.   3 TO 7 P. M.

Ann Blyth

will sing a group of songs
at 4:30 p.m.

During my first year at the Art Gallery of Ontario in 2018, I came across a luminous and mysterious abstract painting in the vaults called *Improvisation No. 2* by Edna Taçon. When I asked my friend, sculptor Carl Taçon, if he knew this artist, he responded: "She's my grandmother." Compelled by the lyricism of the painting and surprised by how little information was available on Edna Taçon, I began my research journey. In the eight years since, her family has provided unwavering dedication and support to this exhibition and catalogue.

My essay (pp. 13–69) charts Edna Taçon's career chronologically and builds on her student years in Toronto to focus specifically on her non-objective art from the 1940s, and how the embodied practice of music inspired her as a visual artist. I have given particular focus to the radicality of Taçon's non-objective practice in Toronto as well as to her lived reality—specifically how she negotiated the duality of living and working in both Canada and the United States while overcoming harmful societal and familial barriers. A very special thanks to Paul, Susan, Carl, and Claire Taçon for sharing recollections, answering countless questions, and lending crucial artworks and archival materials to the exhibition. I am particularly indebted to Carl, who has contributed to this publication a profoundly personal interview (pp. 77–89) about his grandmother that brings her character to life.

Art historian Joyce Zemans was the first to foreground Taçon as the leading practitioner of non-objective art in Canada, and her catalytic 1987 exhibition catalogue about Kathleen Munn and Edna Taçon has been a vital resource for this project. My sincere thanks to Joyce for being a crucial mentor and generous collaborator. Another major source of information and inspiration was a two-day research symposium at the AGO on March 3 and 4, 2025. Organized expertly by Emily Coneybeare, Curatorial Research Intern, the Edna Taçon Study Days gathered curators, artists, and art historians from across North America alongside AGO staff and members of the artist's family to share insights about Taçon's life and the historical contexts in which she worked. Memorably, Toronto violinist Sienna (MinKyong) Cho gave a solo performance, which inspired us to consider Taçon as a musician and to imagine a soundtrack to her paintings in real time. My deep gratitude extends to all who attended the Study Days, especially the presenters: Oliver Botar, Lidia Ferrara, Amy Furness, Anna Hudson, Judith Nasby, Michael Parke-Taylor, and Adam Welch.

The realization of a catalogue of this magnitude is made possible by the efforts of many skilled individuals and colleagues at the AGO. I have deep gratitude for the ever-supportive Georgiana Uhlyarik, Fredrik S. Eaton Curator, Canadian Art, in addition to Curatorial Coordinators Tammy Law and Chloé Wittes for their encouragement and insights. Amy Furness, formerly Rosamond Ivey Special Collections Archivist and Head, Library & Archives, was a key thought partner, and I am grateful for our conversations and trips to Elora to visit the Taçons in tandem. For their leadership and logistical expertise, I extend my appreciation to Jessica Bright, Chief, Exhibitions, Collections & Conservation; Laura Comerford, Director, Exhibitions; and Hillary Taylor, Project Manager. A heartfelt thanks to conservators Meaghan Monaghan, Melissa Potter, and Tessa Thomas for their deft treatments and analyses as well as my dedicated collaborators in Publishing, Jim Shedden, Robyn Lew, and Nives Hajdin-Rorabeck, along with graphic designer, Alina Skyson, for her vision and enthusiasm. Additionally, there are numerous incredible members of the registration and installation teams that have made this exhibition a reality, including Craig Boyko, Scott Cameron, Corrine Carlson, Brent Roe, and Darla Yorston. Sincere thanks to my researcher and accomplice Patricia Ritacca, and steadfast graduate students Emily Coneybeare and Kimberley Rush-Duyguluer, who fact-checked and quested tirelessly for information about Edna Taçon, in addition to Al Stanton-Hagan, Archivist, Edward P. Taylor Library & Archives, for their invaluable support in verifying objects and assorted documentation. I am grateful to David Max Horowitz for his camaraderie and efforts in providing access to the Guggenheim's collection and archives. Julian Cox and Stephan Jost, thank you sincerely for your ongoing guidance and support on this project. Most of all, I honour Edna Taçon: her artistic vision, her humour, her perseverance, and her strength.

Renée van der Avoïrd
Associate Curator, Canadian Art

Written in memory of my cherished friend,
Nicole (Van Zutphen) Audette (1985–2025)

Renée van der Avoird

Verve and Decorum:
The Non-Objective Art
of Edna Taçon

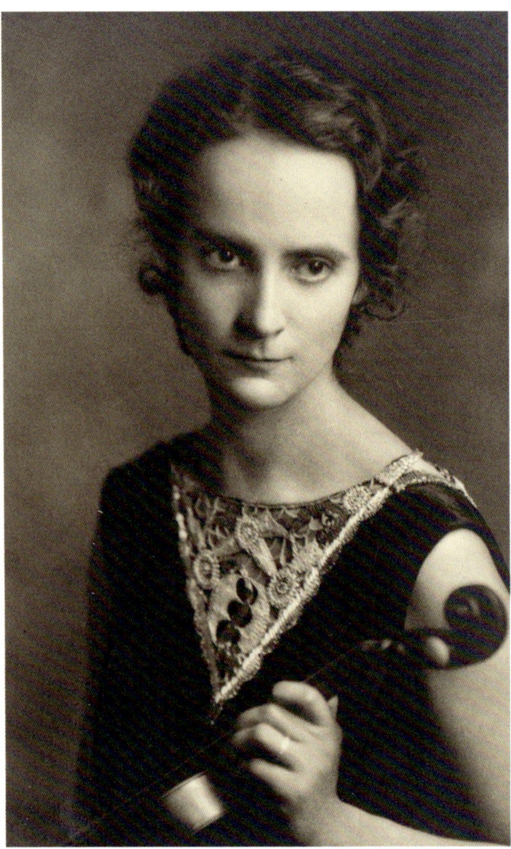

On New Year's Day in 1925, nineteen-year-old Edna Taçon[1] listed ten resolutions in her diary. The first entry read: "To accomplish something every day and not to waste my time. In other words—to work hard."[2] Her strong work ethic is recorded in her diaries, which provide a nuanced understanding of her formative years in Toronto and detail the excitement she experienced in the city. Tea at the Palm Room and concerts at Massey Hall peppered her calendar. She enjoyed shopping at Eaton's Arcade for clothing (nighties, fur coats, galoshes, dress buckles, and blouses), and then would be faced with the ordeal of navigating Toronto's public transit: "Came home at 5 in the streetcar and by the time I reached St. George St. I scarce had a breath left, the car was so jammed! Whew!"[3] Earnest and unfiltered, Taçon's writing also reveals personal hardships and heartache. She grappled with the loss of her parents and endured a tumultuous relationship with artist-teacher Percy Taçon, whom she would marry in 1929.

Taçon studied music at the Hambourg Conservatory and the University of Toronto[4] while she lived at 52 St. George Street. Every day, she dedicated hours to practising piano and violin, attending "leçons" (as she called her lessons) and recitals. Studying in Toronto enriched her creative spirit, and her practice of music led to her non-objective art style that emerged in the 1940s. At that time, Taçon's position as a non-objective artist was a radical one—in fact, she was a leading proponent of the movement in Canada.

Later in life, her other labours and creative strategies—shop-window design, fashion, mural-painting, and teaching—would contribute to her overall impact and legacy as a visual artist. Although little-known today, Taçon succeeded professionally during her lifetime, overcoming societal barriers and a painful, restrictive family life. She navigated the duality of living and working in both Toronto and New York—simultaneously Canadian and American—and experienced a profound entanglement of her identity as a professional musician, artist, student, teacher, wife, mother, and woman in a male-dominated field.

Outbursts of the Soul: From Music to Painting

Student Years

"The artist is working out a theme all the time. Just as an orchestra produces a symphony through sound, non-objective art produces a symphony through colour."—Edna Taçon[5]

Before her career as a painter, Edna Taçon was an accomplished concert violinist. Her early diaries, dating from 1924 to 1929, focus on music. They illustrate a high

1. Born Edna Jeanette MacDougall in 1905, she later went by the last name MacFarlane, sometimes spelled "McFarlane" or misspelled "McFarland," during her student years.

2. Edna Taçon, Diary #1, 1924–25, Taçon family archive.

3. Ibid.

4. It was not uncommon for women to enroll in the University of Toronto's Faculty of Music in the 1920s. In her 1926–27 class list, Taçon was one of thirty-nine women in the faculty of sixty-one students.

5. "Between You and Me," *The Evening Telegram* (November 14, 1941).

6. Taçon, Diary #1, 1924–25.

7. Taçon, Diary #2, 1929, Taçon family archive.

8. Taçon, Diary #1, 1924–25.

9. Ibid.

10. As a means of counteracting the Surrealist movement, this association of artists promoted abstraction through group exhibitions from 1931 to 1936. The practices of *Abstraction-Création* artists varied widely. Artists associated with the group included Piet Mondrian, Barbara Hepworth, and Wassily Kandinsky.

11. Joyce Zemans, Notes from interview with Paul Taçon, October 5, 1987. York University Libraries, Clara Thomas Archives & Special Collections, Joyce Zemans fonds, F0765.

level of discipline, dedication, and self-awareness that would later serve Taçon as a painter; it was clear that she valued the hard work of musicianship and was invigorated by performance during this period. After a public concert in 1925, she rejoiced: "I didn't get panicky as I usually do and felt very much at home—oh! My heart just seemed to grow larger and I could have played forever."[6] Later, she reflected on her inspiration while practising: "I am working with great zest at [Édouardo] Lalo's rhythmical *Symphonie espagnole*...the piece is fairly alive and dancing for me."[7] Taçon also attended important concerts during her student years. "Tomorrow we are going to hear [Jascha] Heifetz...a night of joy and anticipation.... I am almost too excited to write—Heifetz, the loftiest of the violin world, gave me an evening of great beauty and music. He autographed our programs."[8]

She may have initially been drawn to music because her father, Richard MacDougall, played violin to accompany films at vaudeville theatres in Milwaukee, Wisconsin, where Taçon was born. Her father died of tuberculosis and pneumonia when she was six, and her mother, Mathilda Marshall, was unable to provide for her daughter. Taçon was adopted by Jane MacFarlane, a Scottish-born Presbyterian from Goderich, Ontario, who encouraged Taçon's musical talents. Playing the violin from a young age, Taçon, with MacFarlane, moved to Toronto in 1924 to study music.

Professional musicians, some of whom were her professors, played an important role in Taçon's life. Of her instructor violinist Ferdinand Fillion, she wrote: "He has always seemed a father to me—in fact the only one I have known as he is so interested in how I succeed."[9] Other mentors included respected musicians and conductors Géza de Kresz, Sir Ernest MacMillan, Louis Persinger, William Primrose, and Nathan Milstein. After her studies, Taçon played concerts professionally, travelling throughout Ontario and to New York. In 1929, she married Percy Henry Taçon (1902–1983) following a four-year engagement. The couple settled in Hamilton, Ontario, where he taught modern languages, art, and art history at the Central Collegiate Institute. Their first son, Paul, was born in 1932 and Taçon continued to play music and pursue her violin education; she studied in Switzerland during the summer of 1935 and in France the following summer. While abroad, she visited galleries to see modern European art, and she may have seen exhibitions by the *Abstraction-Création* association.[10] The Taçons' second son, Peter, was born in 1936.

"The Feminine Outlook"

When it comes to the art Taçon made prior to the 1940s, there is little on record. Paul Taçon has stated that his mother always made art, even when she dedicated herself to her musical career.[11] A 1945 article in Toronto's *Saturday Night* magazine

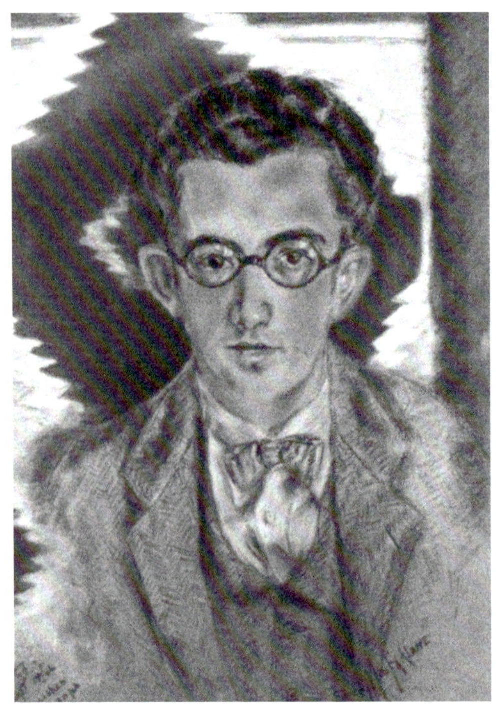

Edna Taçon, *Murray Adaskin*
(black-and-white documentation), 1926

entitled "The Feminine Outlook" reports that she started making art as a child "in order to relax from playing and studying the violin."[12] Taçon's earliest extant artworks include quick caricatures in her diary, such as one of Caesar George Finn (p. 17), a Toronto-based composer, pianist, poet, and "freak in general,"[13] and an early pastel drawing of Canadian violinist and composer Murray Adaskin (left). It is clear, though, that until the mid-1930s, Taçon was intently focused on her music career. Paul Taçon has noted that she did not continue as a musician due to a lack of money for lessons and the quality of violin necessary for her level, in addition to the cost of living part time in New York.[14] When Peter was born, it became increasingly difficult to practise violin, and at home it was easier to make artwork.[15]

Throughout the 1940s, Taçon's marriage and work ethic were often noted in the press ("her working day spans into hours that would horrify any union member").[16] She was often compared to her husband, and the couple was described as a team that skillfully balanced art with domesticity. In a 1941 *Globe and Mail* article, art critic Pearl McCarthy—who would eventually become Taçon's most important champion in the press—remarked: "Their artistic virtues are so different, even when they work in the same medium and 'school,' that there is no competition.... Whether they are sending a conservative still life to the academy, as Mr. Taçon is doing, or exhibiting paper pasted on paper in non-objective art, as Edna Taçon is doing."[17] The following year, McCarthy noted: "In addition to searching for good books, lecturing, and plying between New York and Ontario, the Taçons manage to run a most domesticated establishment with two lively young sons, and to be epicures minus extravagance, with a deft hand at the stove.... They have the gift of enjoying hard work."[18]

Percy Taçon taught full time, and while Edna played violin abroad, Jane MacFarlane took care of Paul and Peter. Percy could not make the trips, despite wishing to join his wife. While abroad, Edna gathered impressions for Percy but "felt again the rising desire to herself become a painter."[19] In *Saturday Night*, it is stated that Percy was the first to introduce Edna to non-objective painting and critiqued her work. The article adds that Edna gave "the vigorous encouragement she has always received from her husband much of the credit for her success as an artist."[20]

As Edna Taçon's career progressed and her reputation as the leading Canadian non-objective artist solidified, Percy also made abstract work and exhibited at the Museum of Non-Objective Painting (MNOP, now the Solomon R. Guggenheim Museum) in two group shows in 1942. He received less attention in the press, however, and ultimately did not achieve a similar level of artistic success to his wife. Paul has noted that Percy may have been simultaneously proud and resentful of Edna's achievements, as he himself never developed a fully personal style.[21] Edna's diaries from as early as 1924 reveal tension in her

12. Ann Foster, "The Feminine Outlook:
    Edna Taçon: Pioneer in Esoteric Art of
    Non-objective Painting," *Saturday Night*
    (November 24, 1945).

13. Taçon, Diary #2, 1929.

14. Zemans, Notes from interview with
    Paul Taçon.

15. Foster, "The Feminine Outlook."

16. Ibid.

17. Pearl McCarthy, "Art and Artists,"
    The Globe and Mail (November 1, 1941).

18. Pearl McCarthy, "Art and Artists: Abstract
    Art in New Exhibit," *The Globe and Mail*
    (November 5, 1942).

19. Ibid.

20. Foster, "The Feminine Outlook."

21. Zemans, Notes from interview with
    Paul Taçon.

22. Foster, "The Feminine Outlook."

relationship with Percy, and entries beginning in 1930 detail the acute physical and psychological abuse that he inflicted on her. However, as her public profile grew, Edna maintained in the press that their marriage was a happy and productive one—except for a 1945 reflection on her engagement to Percy: "I was certain in those days that two artists couldn't live happily together, and that if I began to paint seriously it would wreck our marriage!"[22]

"Music-Pictures"

If Edna Taçon's husband introduced her to non-objective art in the late 1930s, she was also almost certainly aware of trends in abstract art independently of him. Although not recorded in her diary, she likely visited the International Exhibition of Modern Art, organized by *Société Anonyme* in 1927 at the Art Gallery of Toronto (AGT, now the Art Gallery of Ontario), which was championed by pivotal Canadian painter Lawren Harris (1885–1970) and included more than 151 works by 106 artists from 22 countries, including Fernand Léger (1881–1955), Max Ernst (1891–1976), László Moholy-Nagy (1895–1946), and Wassily Kandinsky

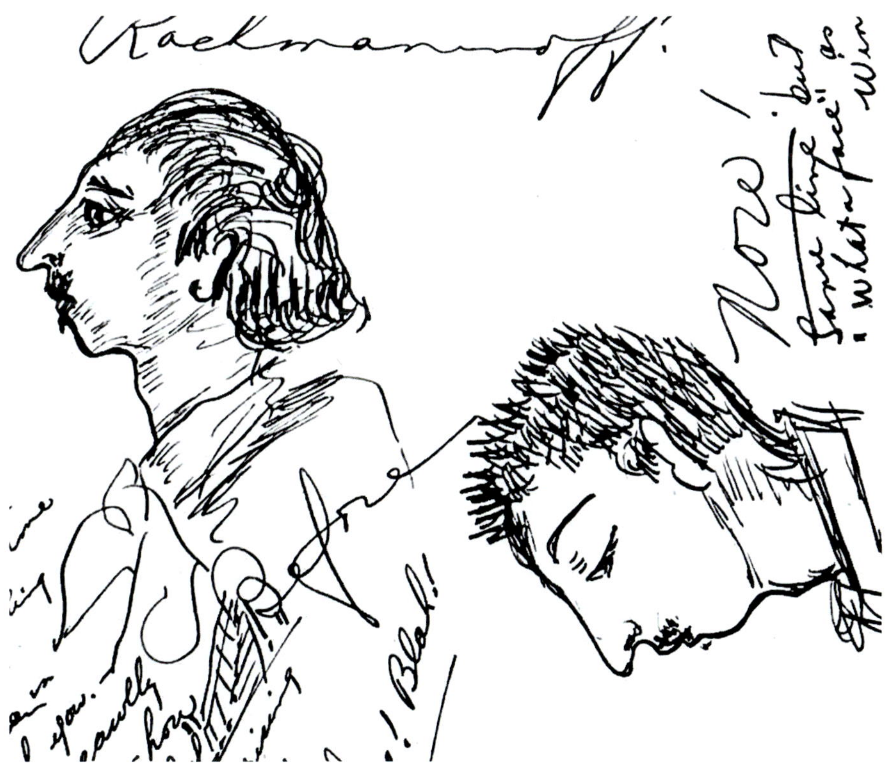

Edna Taçon, *Caricature of Caesar George Finn,* January 14, 1929

23. Judith Nasby, *Rolph Scarlett: Painter, Designer, Jeweller* (McGill-Queen's University Press, 2004), 63.

24. Joyce Zemans, *Kathleen Munn and Edna Taçon: New Perspectives on Modernism in Canada* (Art Gallery of York University, 1988), note 16, 48.

(1866–1944) (below). Marking the first time abstract art was shown in Canada, the exhibition was considered scandalous in the extensive press coverage it received. Another influential exhibition Taçon may have seen at the AGT is the 1937 Canadian Group of Painters' exhibition, which included four abstract works by Lawren Harris.

While visiting New York for violin concerts throughout the 1920s and '30s, Taçon also likely saw work by non-objective painters such as Kandinsky and Rudolf Bauer (1889–1953). When the MNOP opened in 1939, Guelph, Ontario-born artist Rolph Scarlett (1889–1984)—whom the Taçons knew from social circles in Ontario—exhibited there and helped Edna integrate into the MNOP community.[23] As well, Harris exhibited in the MNOP loan exhibitions during the spring and summer of 1940; Harris's work, as well as Scarlett's, likely influenced Taçon's decision to approach the museum in the first place.[24]

The influence of non-objective artists like Kandinsky can be detected in Taçon's work: geometric forms, invented shapes, and colour that she described as "a means of expressing the inner life—call it soul, spirit, or mind...all conditions and

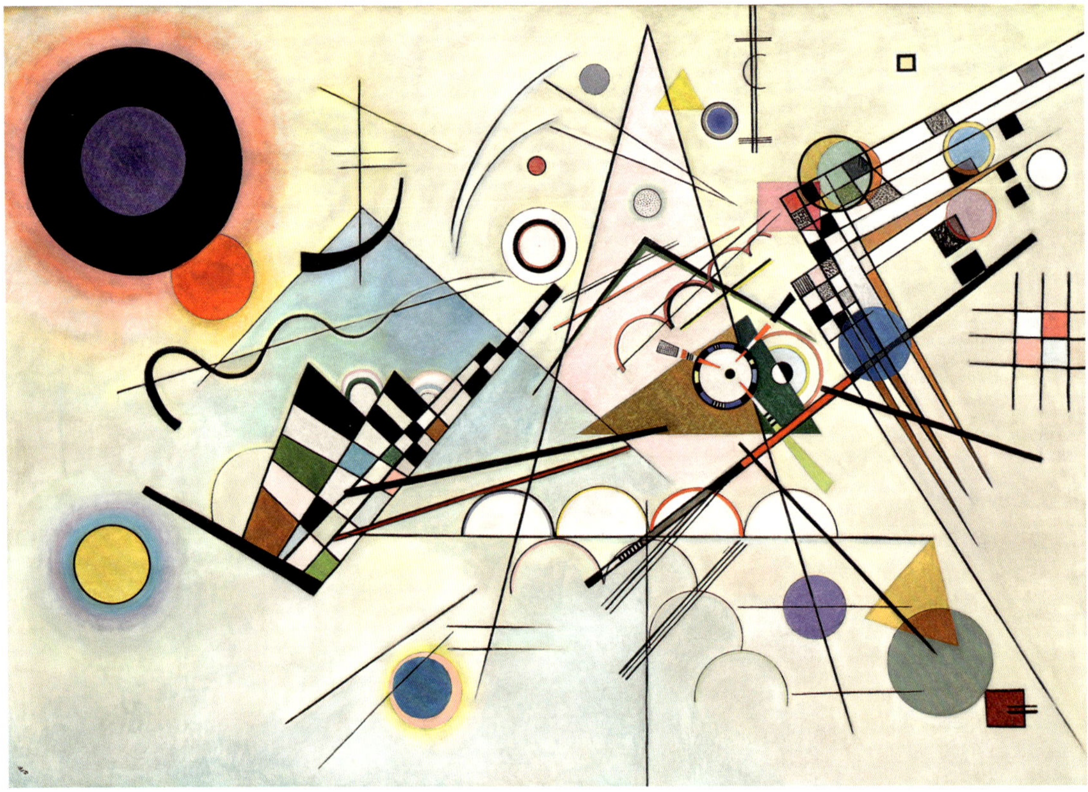

Wassily Kandinsky, *Composition 8 (Komposition 8)*, 1923

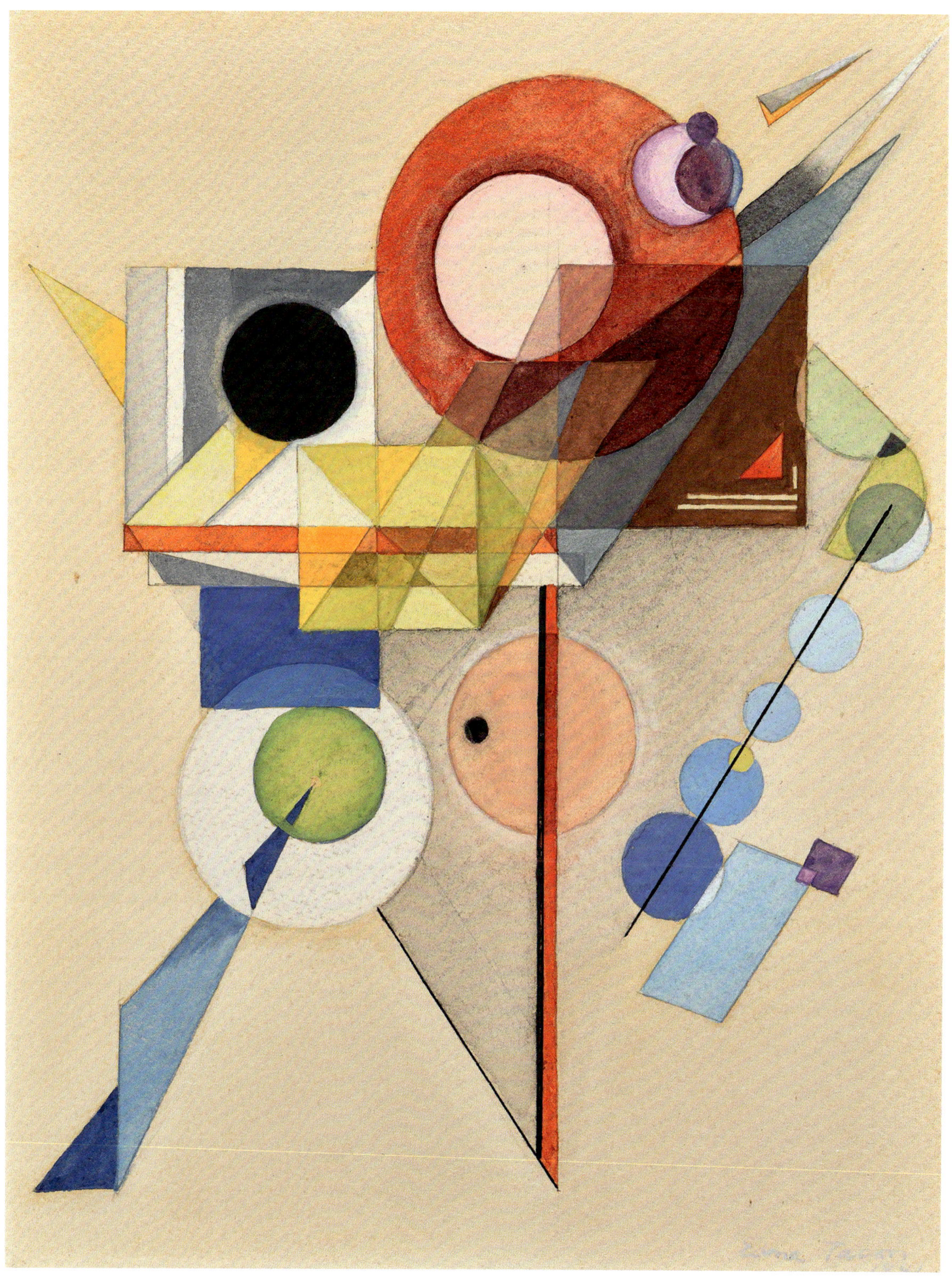

"UNTITLED" 1941

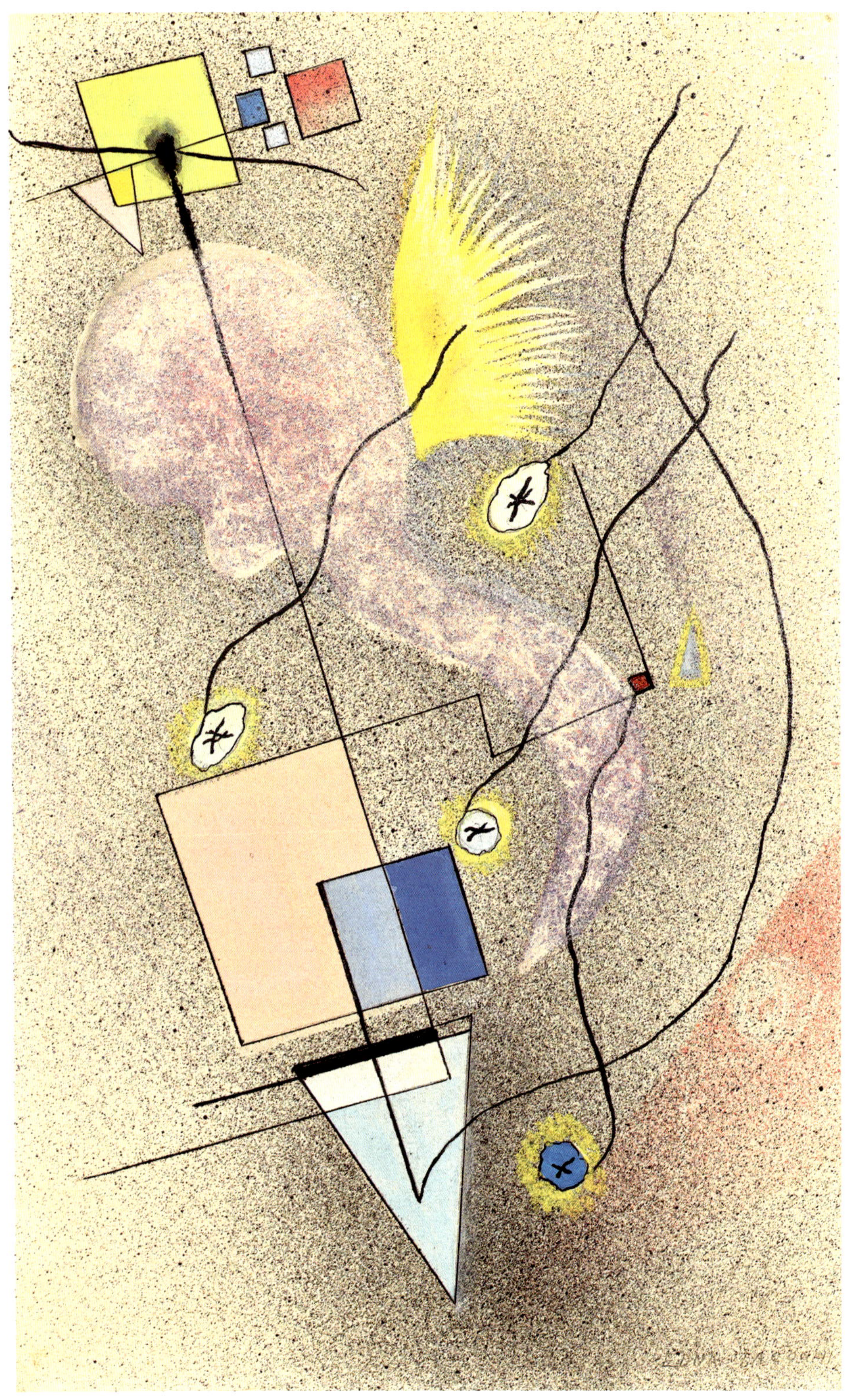

"UNTITLED" 1941   20

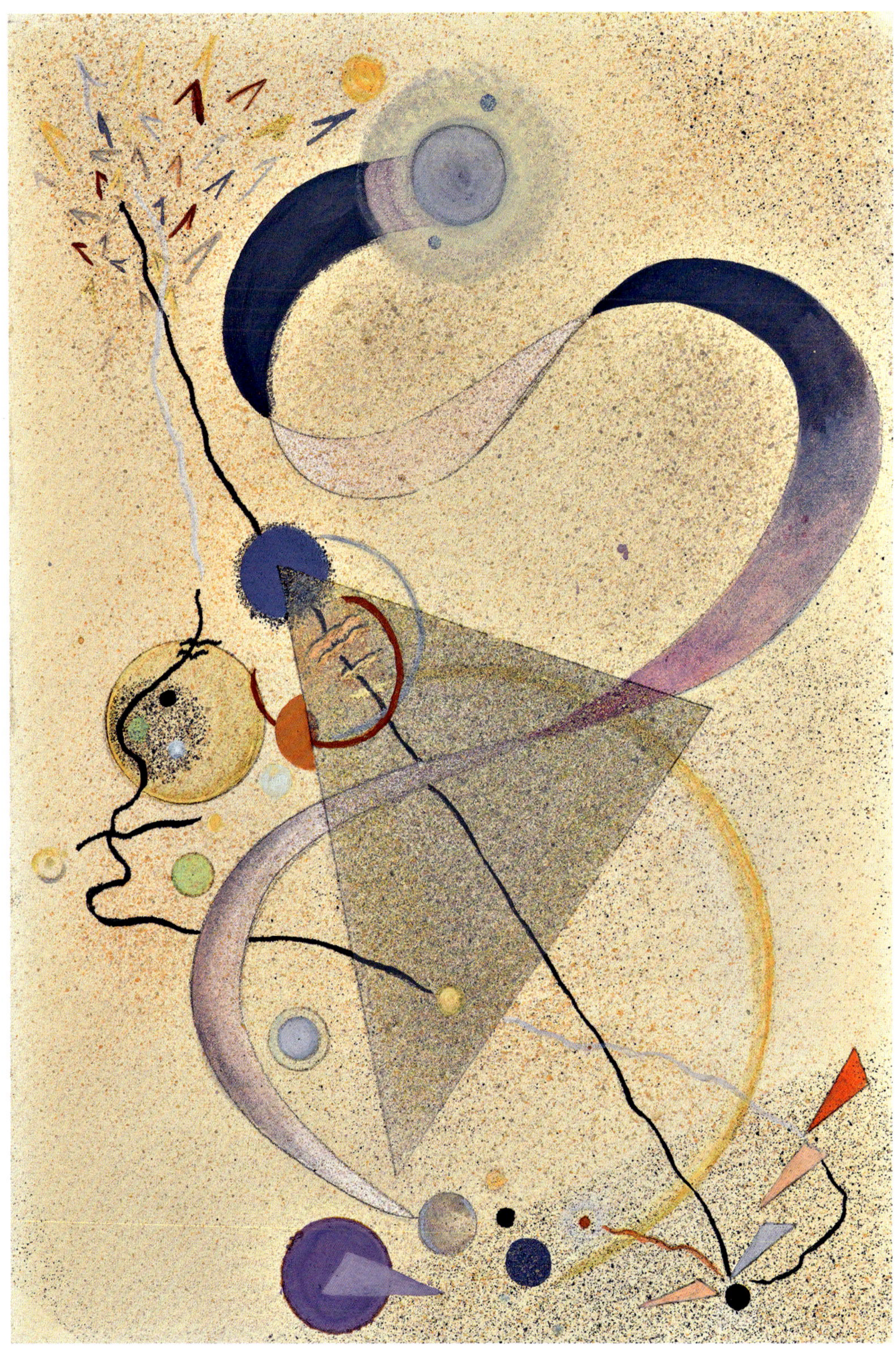

21

"UNTITLED" c. 1941

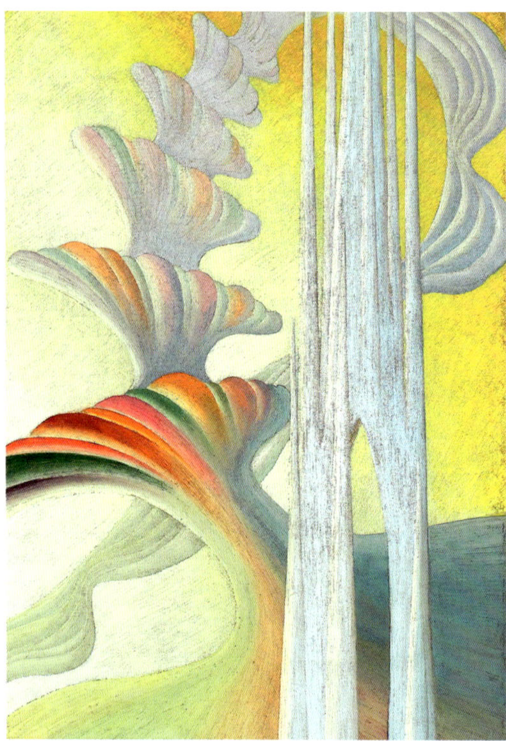

outbursts of the soul."[25] The MNOP was dedicated to strengthening parallels between music and art; the museum played classical music by composers such as Mozart and Bach in the galleries, a practice in line with Kandinsky's theories.[26] Hilla Rebay[27] (1890–1967), MNOP co-founder and its first director, employed music and other sensory and design strategies—incense, walls decorated with pleated grey velour, and grey carpeted floors—to foster a contemplative environ-ment for visitors to experience non-objective art, all of which stemmed from the spiritual movement of theosophy.[28]

Another point of connection between non-objective art and music is titling. Kandinsky and his contemporaries often titled their non-objective paintings with musical terms such as *Improvisation* and *Composition*. Many of Taçon's titles, too, reference music, and in describing her work she often used the allegory of music, especially when explaining concepts of non-objective art. She has stated that "just as an orchestra produces a symphony through sound, non-objective art produces a symphony through colour."[29] For Taçon, the synergy between classical music and non-objective painting must have been exceptionally strong—as a professional musician first, she understood music in a profound, embodied way that many of her fellow non-objective painters may not have. Augustus Bridle, music and art critic for the *Toronto Star*, picked up on the artist's specific position as both musician and artist, noting that "Edna Taçon is obviously a music-lover. Her geometrized music-paintings are things of beauty; as color-art [*sic*] and studies of geometric form alone, they're works of art. And any visitor to this show may see a fugue and take it home—without bothering to buy a record, just to be hearing it."[30] In a second article, he mentioned her again: "Miss Taçon's music-pictures—many of which are undeniably beautiful—are more authentic than one in 1,000 painters could possibly portray, because she actually played some of the pictures that she paints."[31]

Canadian artist Bertram Brooker (1888–1955) was similarly interested in Kandinsky and the links between music and painting. It is not clear if Taçon and Brooker knew one another, but they shared the belief that music can offer an escape from physical reality, allowing one to be transported to a world of aesthetic exaltation or ecstasy, such as in Brooker's abstract painting *"Chorale" (Bach)* (left). Like Brooker, Taçon utilized abstraction to explore how visual forms might relate to musical ones. Works such as *Improvisation No. 2* (p. 25) exemplify her power to evoke musical associations or moods through paint. For Taçon, the process of painting, like music, was intuitive and rooted in creative imagination, an embodied choreography of line and colour that is open to each viewer's own interpretation and emotional associations. She once explained: "There has to be intellect behind it, but if you start trying to intellectualize, you miss the whole point of the intuitive search for new delights and satisfactions.... One has to be alone for intense concentration so that the feeling of ecstasy will come out in the paint."[32]

25. "Put on Canvas What They Feel: Edna Taçon, Exponent of Non-Objective Art, Addresses Artists," *The Hamilton Spectator* (December 15, 1944).

26. Kandinsky's *Concerning the Spiritual in Art* (originally published in 1911, with an English translation by Rebay published by the Guggenheim Foundation in 1946) was a pivotal text for Taçon. It calls for a spiritual revolution in painting in which artists focus on expressing their inner selves rather than the material world, similar to how musicians do not depend on the material world for their music.

27. Much like her earlier professional connections with instructors like Ferdinand Fillion, Taçon developed a close relationship with Rebay, who would go on to serve as an important mentor and supporter of her work in New York during the 1940s.

28. The MNOP housed American collector Solomon R. Guggenheim's collection of modern art. Kandinsky formed the nucleus of this collection, with over 150 of his works that were often rotated into exhibitions. For Guggenheim and Rebay, endorsing modern art in America was a radical act, given the turbulent years leading up to and during World War II, during which regionalist art predominated.

29. Taçon quoted in "Between You and Me," *The Evening Telegram* (November 14, 1941).

30. Augustus Bridle, "Look at a Fugue and Take it Home," *Toronto Star* (January 18, 1944).

31. Augustus Bridle, "Music Art, Drama: Artist Paints Music," *Toronto Star* (October 7, 1944).

32. Pearl McCarthy, "Emotions Are Pictured in 'Non-Objective' Art," *The Globe and Mail* (September 26, 1944).

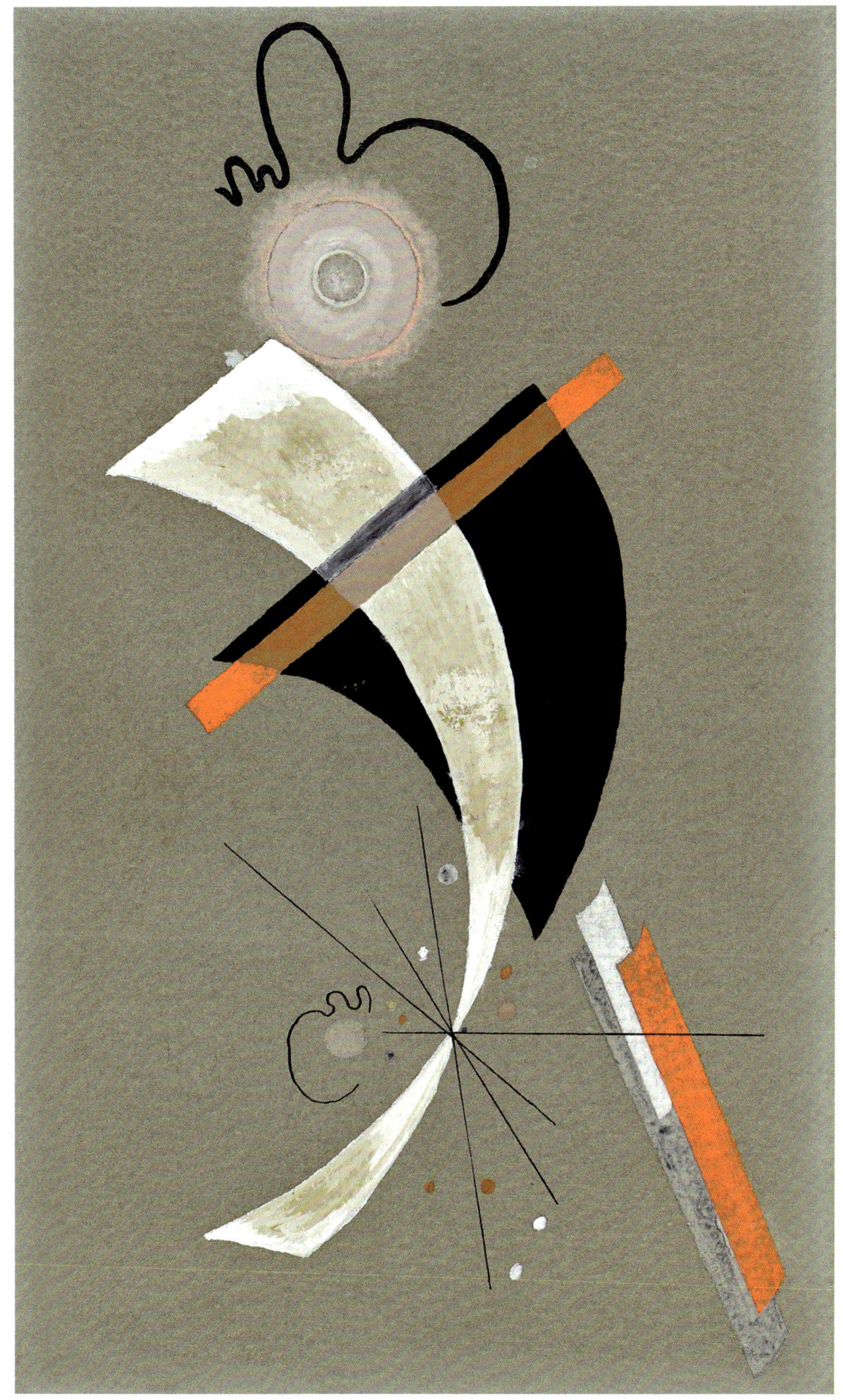

"UNTITLED" c. 1941

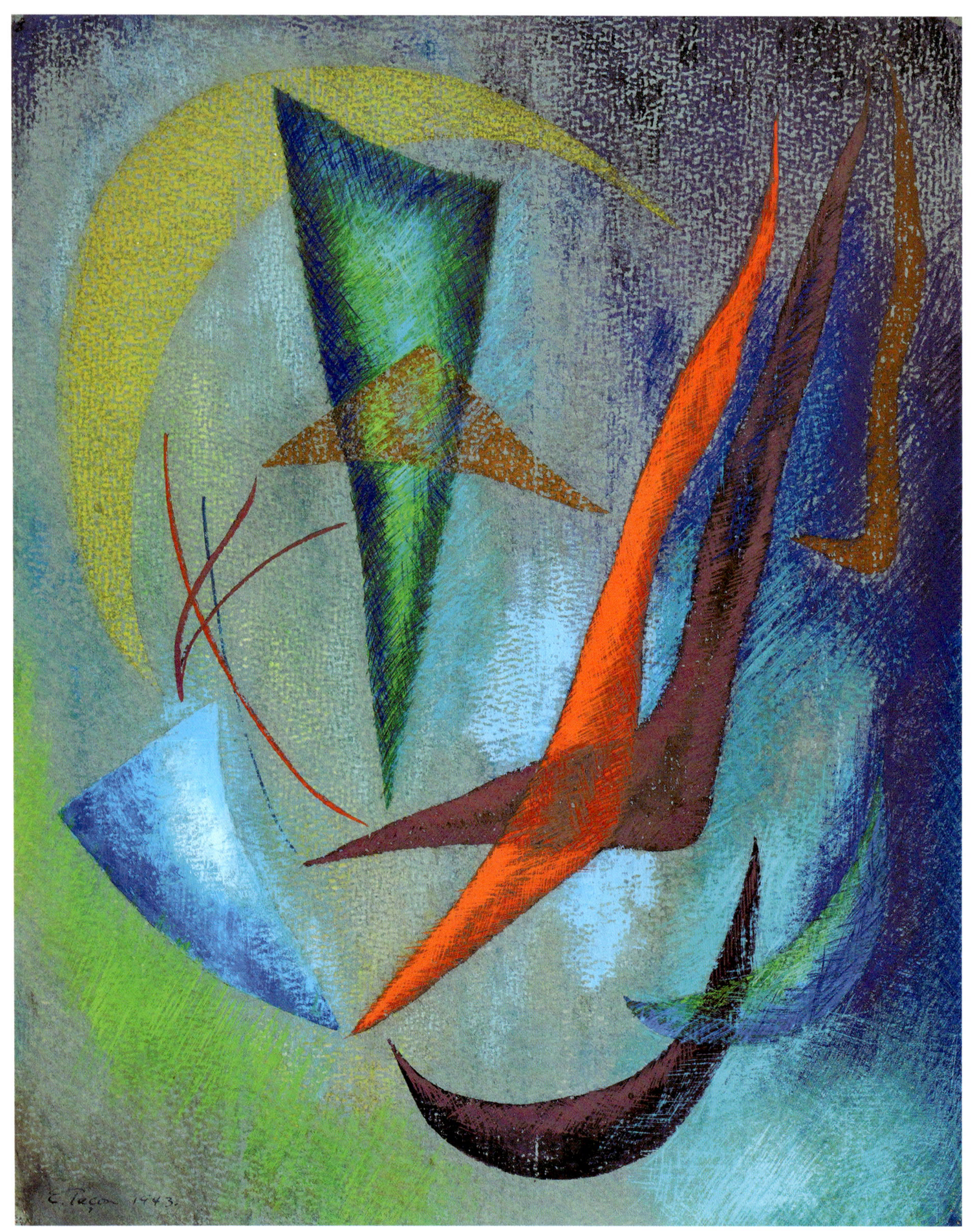

"BLUE NOCTURNE" 1943   24

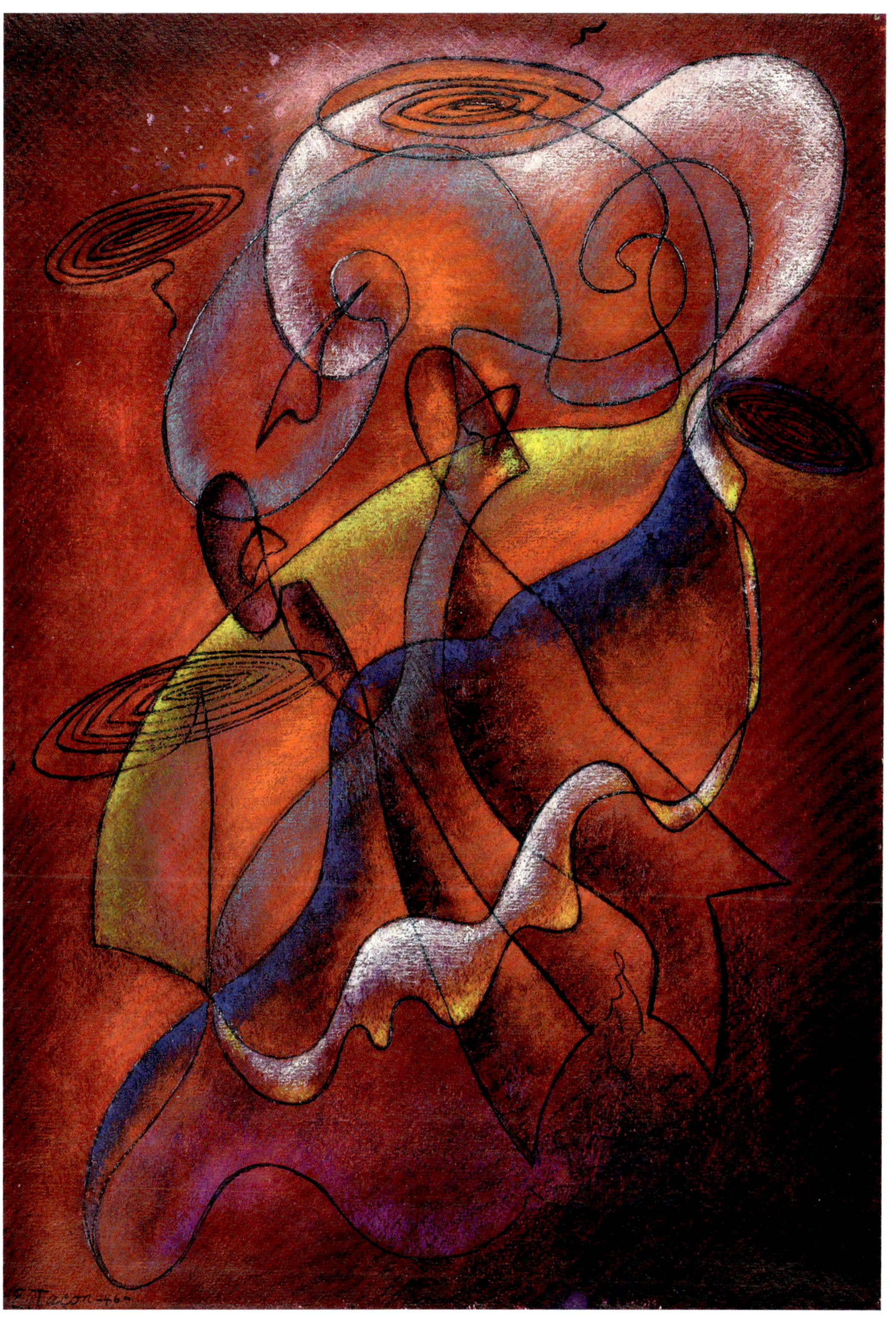

"IMPROVISATION NO. 2" 1946

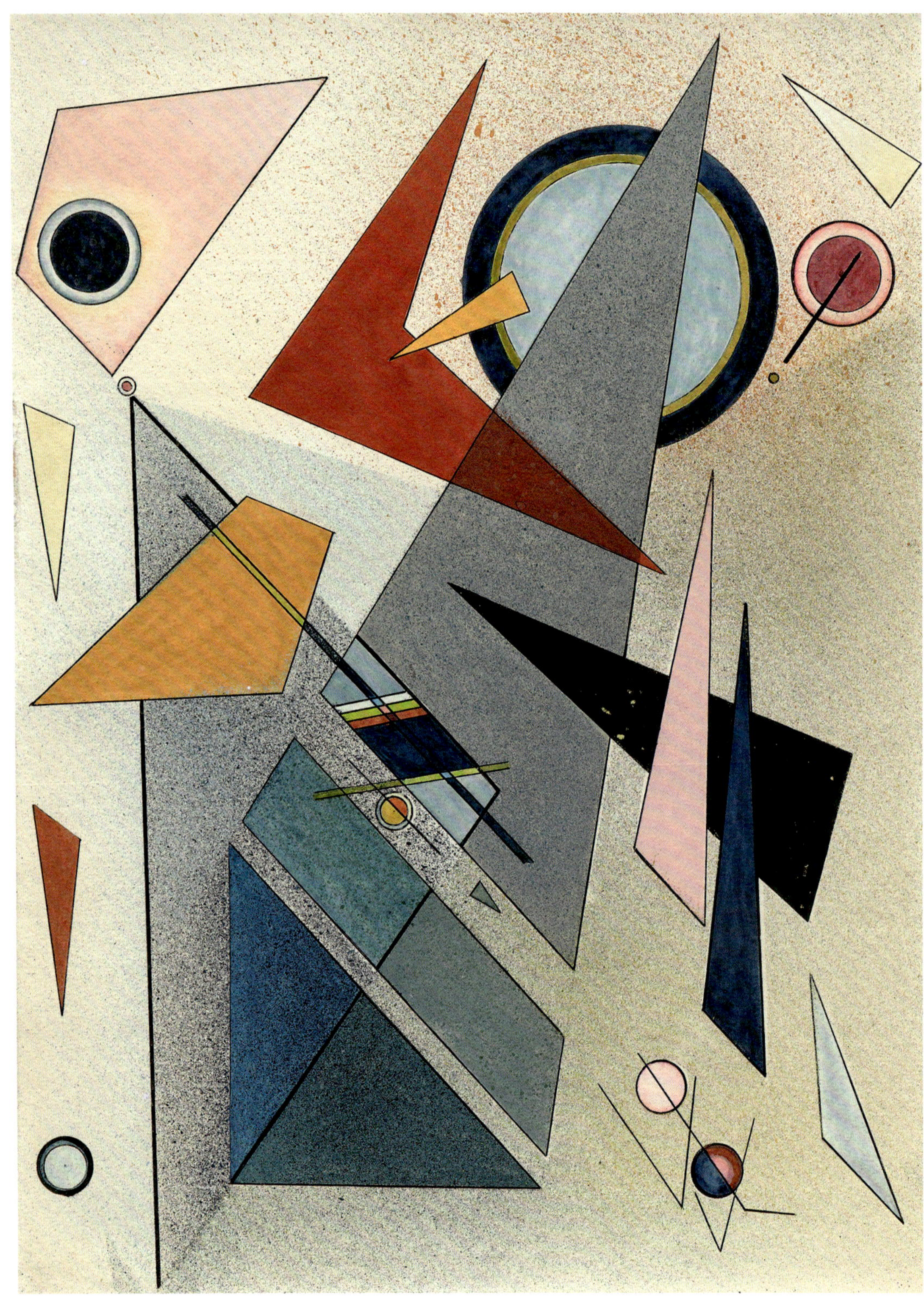

"UNTITLED" c. 1941   26

33. Letter from Taçon to Rebay, November 1940. Guggenheim Museum Archives, A0010-3034-1.

Recent Experiments in Non-Objective Art

Paper Plastics

New York in the 1940s was a hub of radical artistic experimentation. During this turbulent decade, innovative developments led to new styles of art-making inspired by European abstractionists such as Kandinsky, Kazimir Malevich (1879–1935), and Piet Mondrian (1872–1944), and surrealists Max Ernst and André Breton (1896–1966), all of whom had immigrated to New York. The city's art community also included American practitioners like Georgia O'Keeffe (1887–1986) and became known as the global centre for modern art. Taçon, enthralled with New York's creative climate, had developed her distinctive non-objective style, starting with collage. In 1941, she had three exhibitions, which launched her career as a visual artist both in Toronto and New York. *Ten American Non-Objective Painters* at the MNOP opened in March; *Exhibition of Non-Objective Pictures (Paintings & Paper Plastics) by Edna Taçon* at Studio 83 in New York in October; and *Non-Objective Pictures by Edna Taçon* at Eaton's Fine Art Galleries in Toronto in November.

The first exhibition, a group show at the MNOP, resulted from a letter that Taçon wrote in November 1940 to the secretary of Hilla Rebay requesting a meeting to show "some non-objective pictures done in paper medium."[33] Taçon's collages—small, dynamic compositions of intermingling geometric and biomorphic shapes of paper cut from paper sample catalogues—were referred to as "paper plastics," a term Taçon adopted from Rebay. In works like *Primavera* (p. 28), Taçon balanced delicate floating forms with metallic and matte paper colours, evoking gentle movement. In preliminary drawings, she made precise designs for her collages and would then experiment with colours and materials when executing the works. The hybridity of Taçon's controlled yet intuitive approach to collage is evident in *Primavera*, as the elements come together in a harmony that appears to be at once pre-designed and completely natural. Taçon's dexterity, most certainly acquired from playing violin, enabled her to make collages with precision and control. *Magic Carpet* (p. 29) is meticulously composed of dozens of minuscule slices of paper that come together in a dense composition. Unlike most other Taçon collages, *Magic Carpet* bears a title that alludes to a particular subject, one that evokes the artist's enduring interest in symbolism and fantasy.

As per the Guggenheim Foundation's objectives, Rebay offered critiques of all non-objective artwork submitted to the Museum. After reviewing Taçon's collages in 1940, Rebay selected three (all dated 1940) to include in the 1941 loan exhibition that featured nine other artists, including Rolph Scarlett.

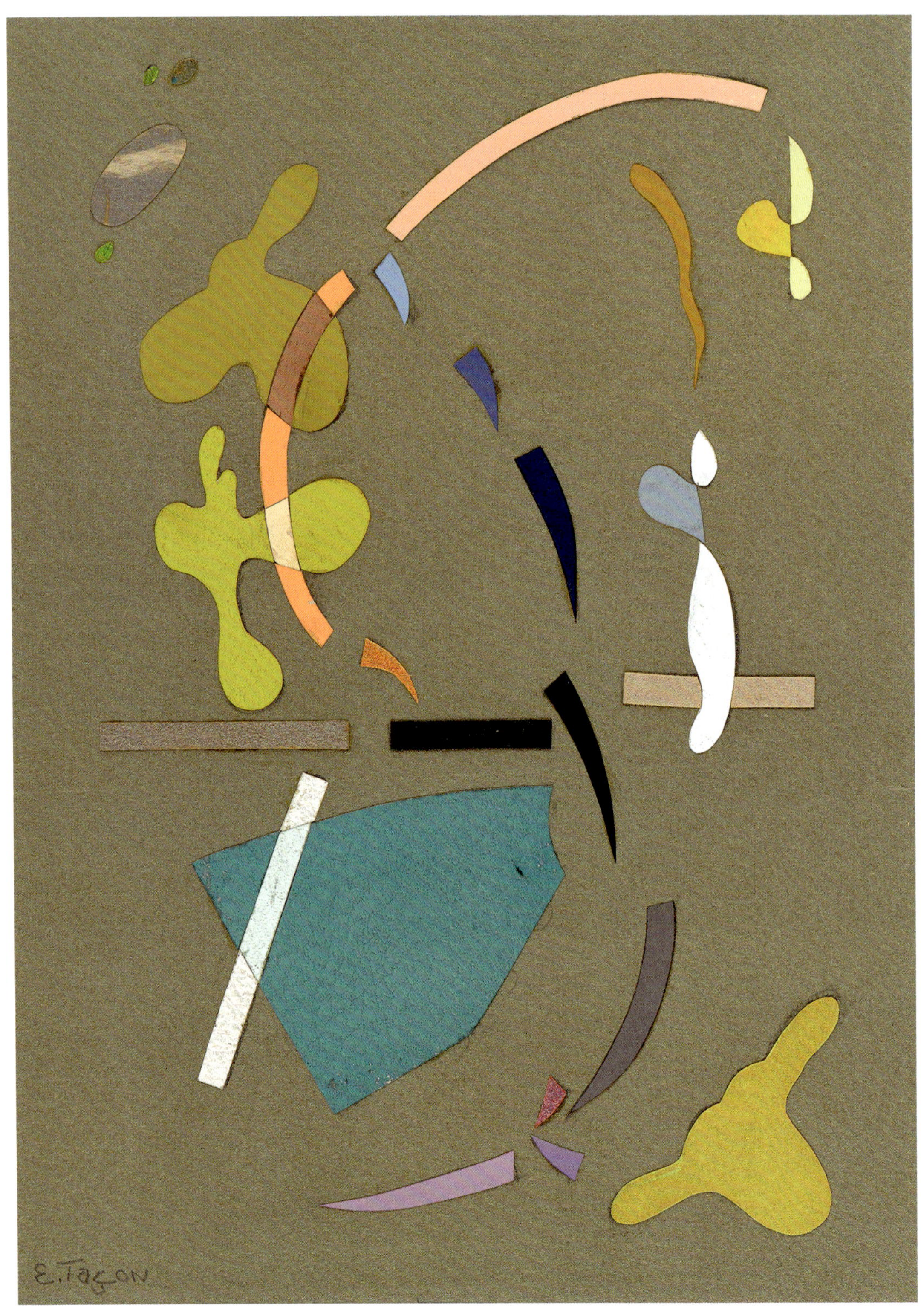

"PRIMAVERA" c. 1940

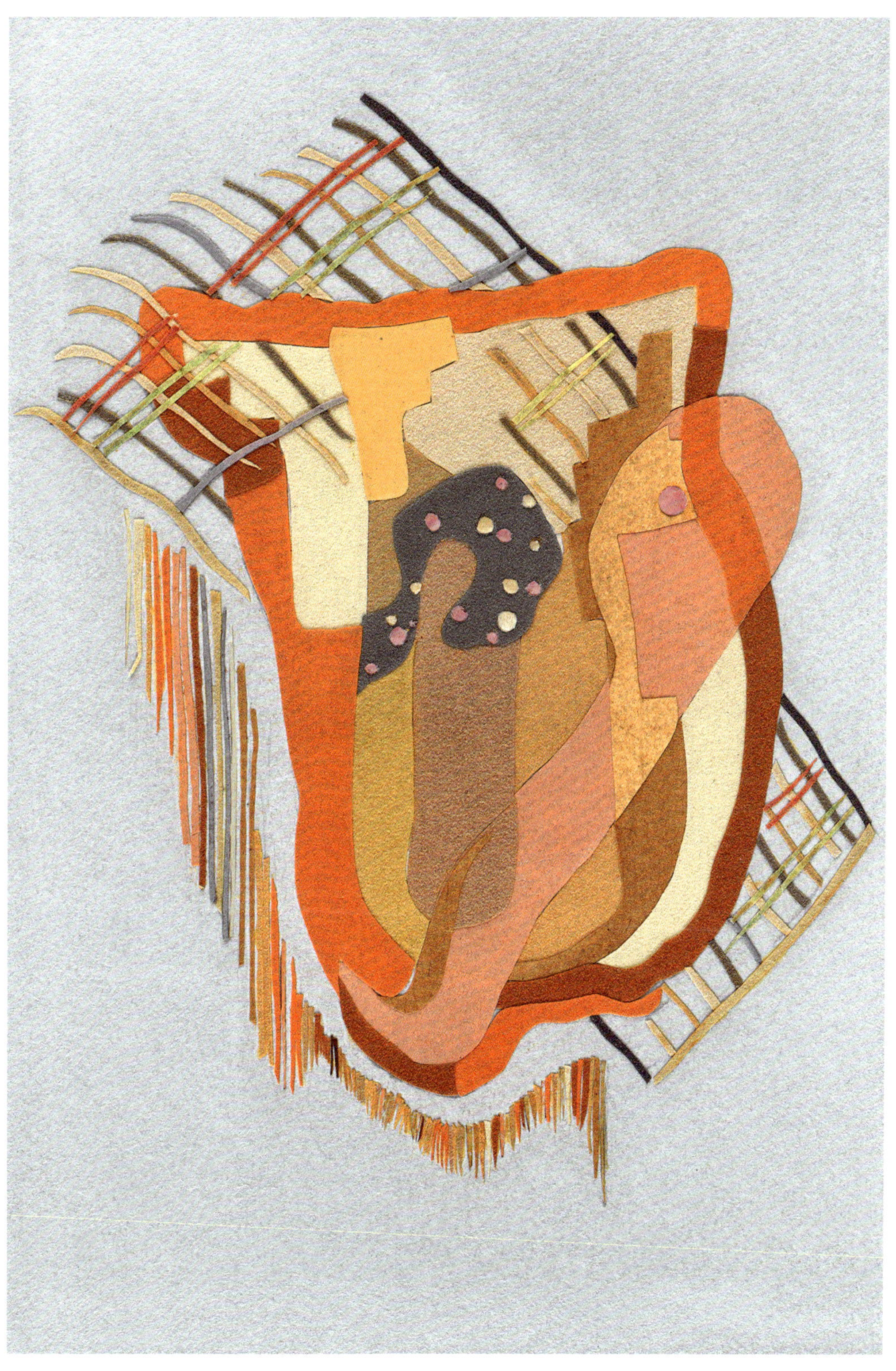

"MAGIC CARPET" c. 1941

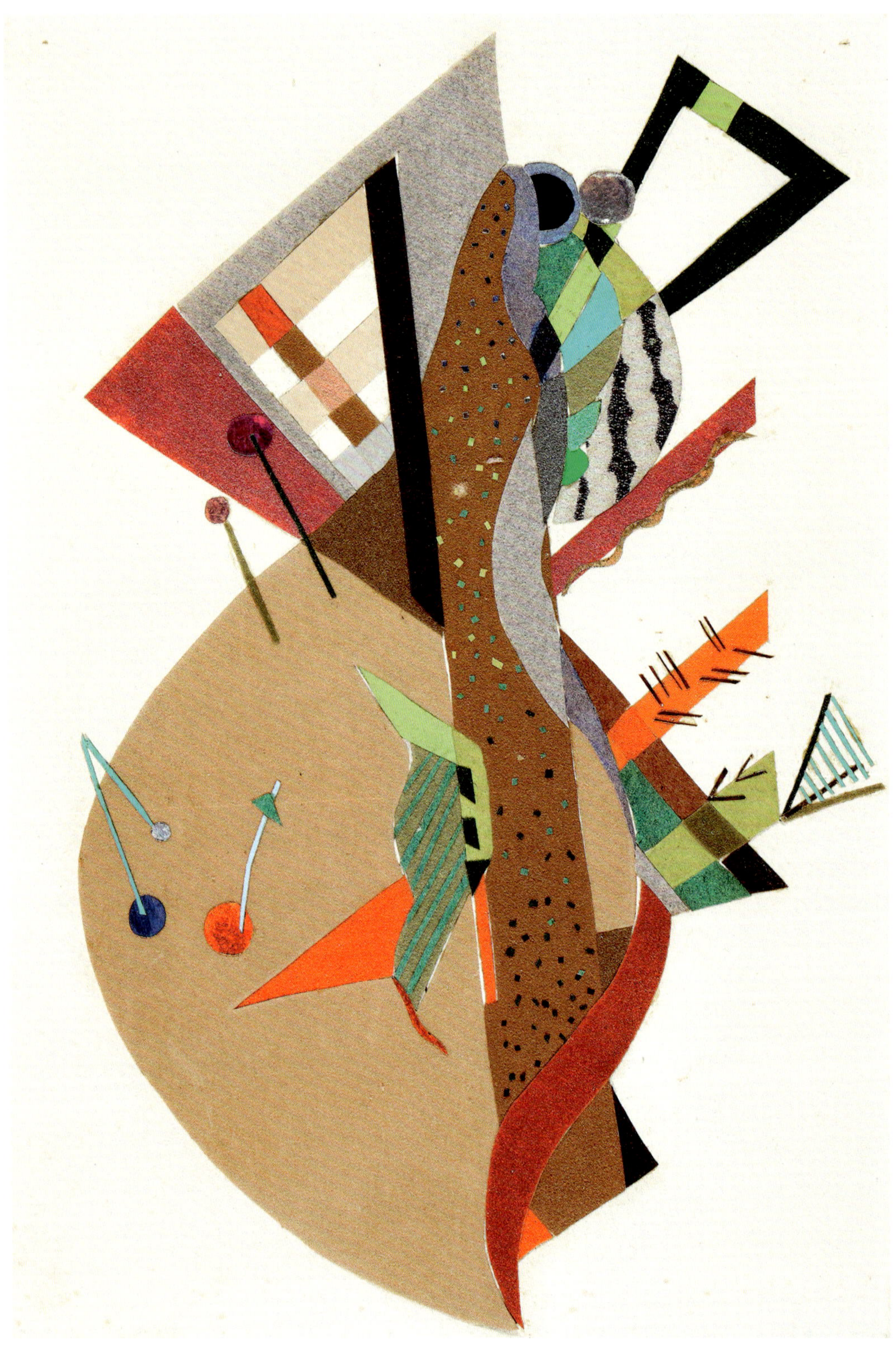

"COMPOSITION" 1940   30

34. "Museum of Non-Objective Art exhibition,"
    ARTnews review, n.d., signed "D.B.,
    April 1–14, 1941."

35. Letter from Taçon to Rebay, March 31,
    1941. Guggenheim Museum Archives,
    A0010-3034-1.

36. Zemans, *New Perspectives on Modernism
    in Canada*, note 16, 48.

37. Karole Vail, *The Museum of Non-Objective
    Painting: Hilla Rebay and the Origins
    of the Solomon R. Guggenheim Museum*
    (The Guggenheim Museum, 2009), 46.

38. Letter from Rebay to Taçon, November 19,
    1942. Guggenheim Museum Archives,
    A0010-3034-1.

ARTnews reviewed the exhibition, singling out Taçon's work and reproducing an image of *Composition* (p. 30): "If the little mezzanine on which they are hung doesn't give you claustrophobia, you might enjoy some of the non-objective pictures by relatively unknown Americans at the Museum of Non-Objective Art [*sic*]. Edna Taçon opens up a bright new world—fresh as an Irishman's dream of Eire on St. Patrick's Day."[34]

Taçon showed her work at the MNOP in eleven exhibitions from 1941 to 1945. During that time, Rebay and Taçon developed a productive, if at times fraught, professional relationship. In 1941, Taçon won a Solomon R. Guggenheim Foundation Scholarship that included three years of comprehensive study and regular stipends called "paint material cheques."[35] As part of its mission, the Foundation subsidized non-objective artists, a policy that was publicized in New York papers such as *Art Digest* and *ARTnews*.[36] A significant number of artists received such payments from the Guggenheim Foundation, often small sums that offered vital assistance in acquiring art supplies.[37] In 1942, Taçon began working at the MNOP. Rebay instructed:

> See that all lavatories are clean, all brass, all floors, faucets, basins, walls, all corners are immaculate. There are no holes made by nail, no unused nails left in the walls, entrance and doors in shape, and a man at door at this post at all times. Tell Miss Autorino and Miss Droitiere to do the same, as men do not see these things as women do.[38]

Taçon was living in New York only part time during this period. She stayed for months at a time at the Winslow Hotel on East 55th Street and then would travel back to her family home at 352 Aberdeen Avenue in Hamilton, Ontario. She likely stayed away from home as long as possible for her own safety and peace of mind, given Percy's abusive behaviour, in addition to the exciting pull of the New York art world. Little is known about the decisions Taçon made to survive and overcome personal trauma, but her artistic drive—as well as her devotion to her sons, as expressed in her many letters to them—fuelled her continuously.

"Hostess" and Designer

In addition to maintaining an immaculate building at the MNOP, Taçon worked as a docent (then called a "hostess"), greeting visitors and touring them through the museum. The hostesses wrote weekly reports about visitors' reactions to the art and MNOP lectures. Taçon reported on many visitors:

> Miss Tournier, musician and pianist, enjoyed a few hours here last Saturday. The first thing that "struck" her when she entered the Museum

39. Taçon, Hostess report, April 7, 1943.
    Guggenheim Museum Archives,
    M0007-148-47-5.

40. Ibid.

41. Letter to Taçon from Rebay, July 17, 1941.
    Guggenheim Museum Archives,
    A0010-3034-1.

42. Letter to Taçon from Rebay, April 20,
    1943. Guggenheim Museum Archives,
    M0007-148-47.

In addition to visitors, some of whom she might have related to, Taçon also met
many like-minded artists who toured, exhibited, and worked at the MNOP. The
ongoing cycle of exhibitions complemented by lectures and group shows on
the mezzanine level provided an opportunity for non-objective artists to discuss
each other's work and exchange ideas. Despite the obvious gender discrimination
in Taçon's workplace, there were numerous women artists exhibiting at the
MNOP in the early 1940s, such as Irene Rice Pereira (1902–1971), Perle Fine
(1905–1988), Alice Trumbull Mason (1904–1971), Alice Mattern (1909–1945),
and Rebay herself.

Taçon's relationship with Rebay was complex, both financially and emotionally. Taçon faced uncertainty while working steadfastly to create her own
exhibition opportunities and had become dependent on Rebay as a patron during
the early 1940s. In a 1941 letter to Taçon, Rebay stated that "the Foundation
will help you for four months more with payments of $40.00 a month when you are
in New York to study" and asked Taçon to "not mention to anyone that you are
being helped by the Foundation, nor to what extent."[41] In a similar missive two years
later, Rebay remarked: "The reason I made Mr. Guggenheim buy something
was to help you out with your doctor bill. So please do not speak; do not mention it,
as it would not have been bought otherwise."[42] The secretive and seemingly
manipulative nature of Rebay's additional support of Taçon indicates a clear power
differential, and that Rebay held a position of authority over Taçon. However,
their correspondence, albeit transactional, reveals a sympathetic closeness. In 1943,
Taçon thanked Rebay for her critiques and praised her lectures, while also
detailing a physical condition she was battling:

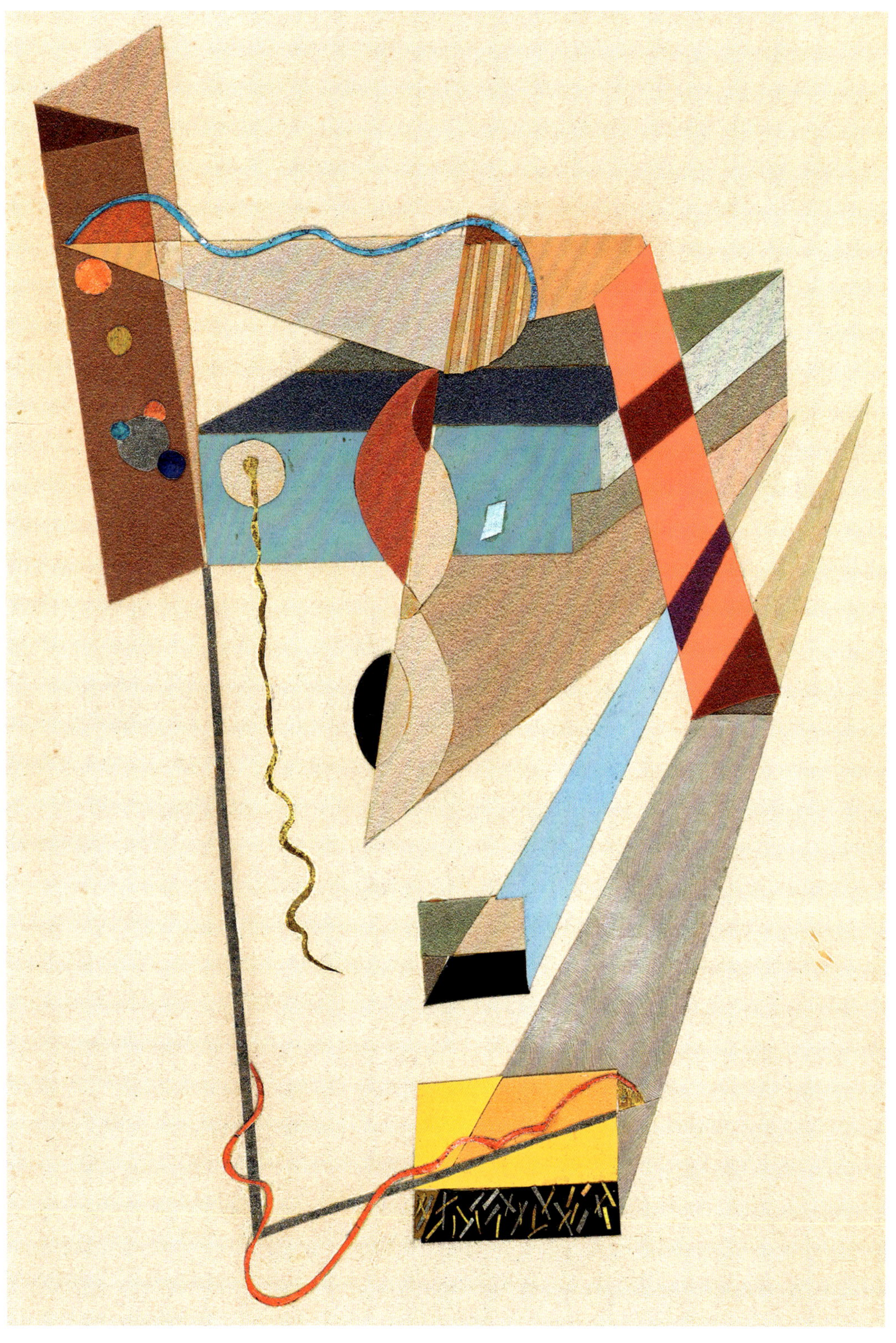

"INVENTION" c. 1941

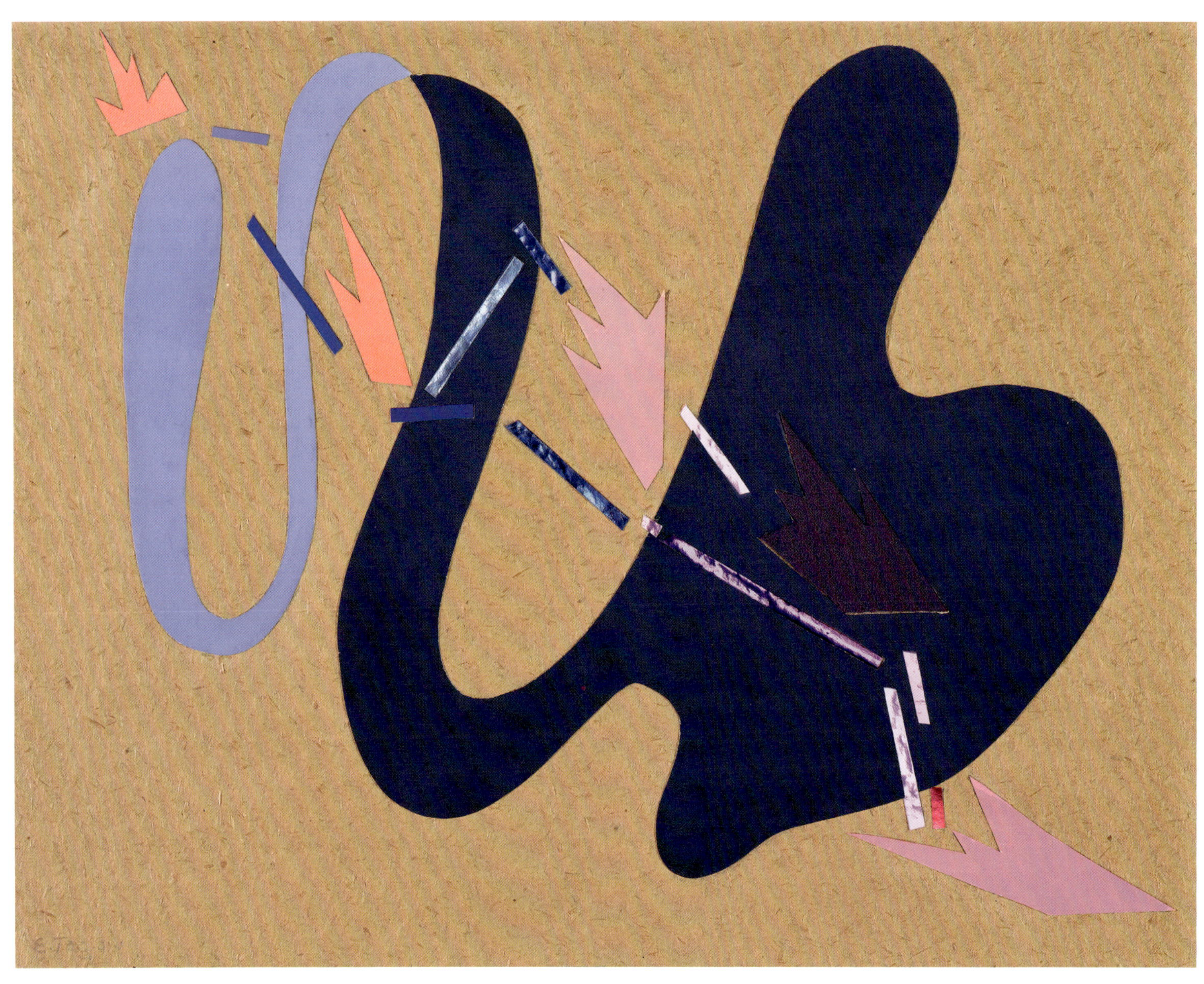

"STUDY IN MOTION" c. 1941   34

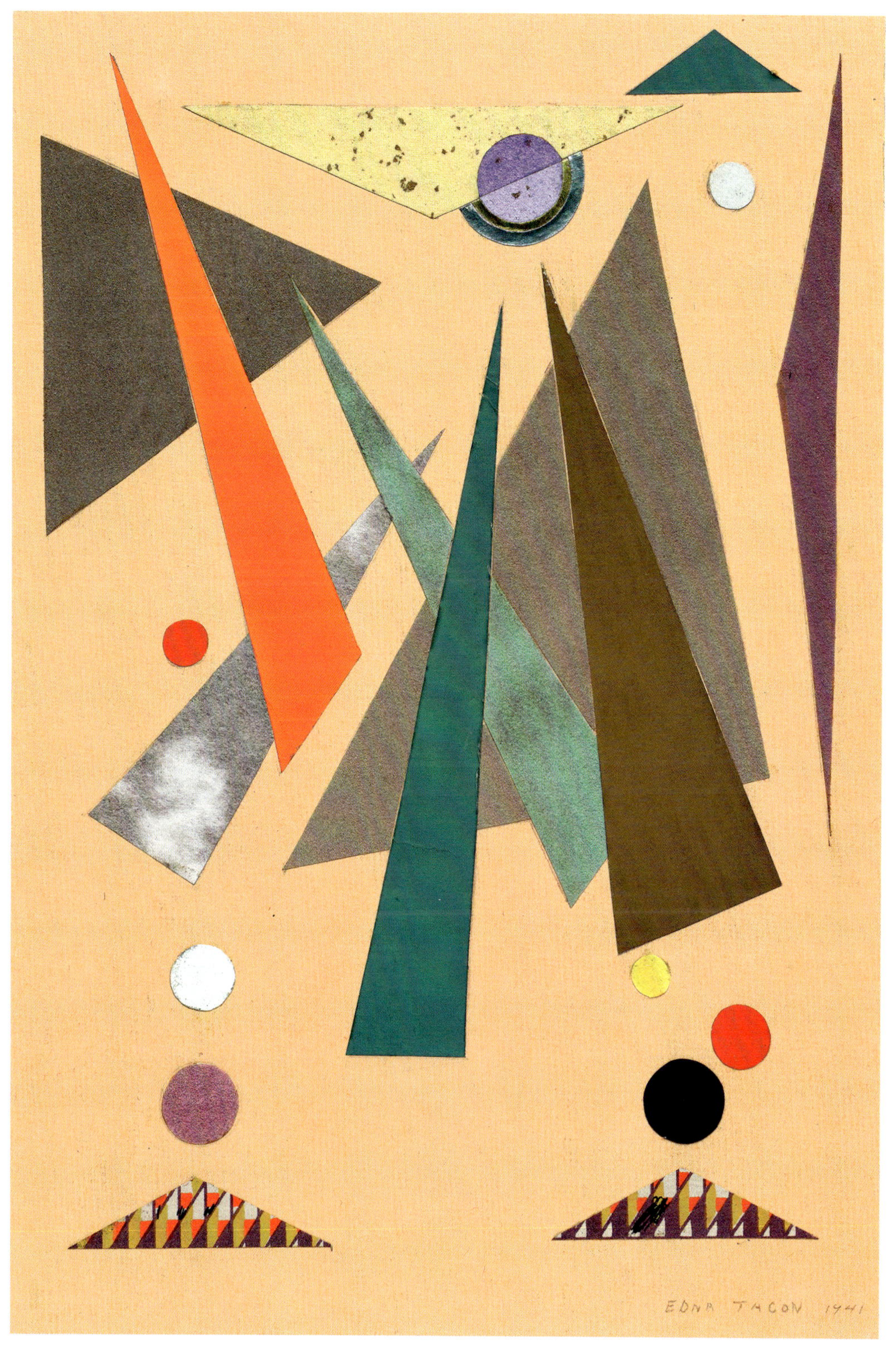

"UNTITLED" 1941

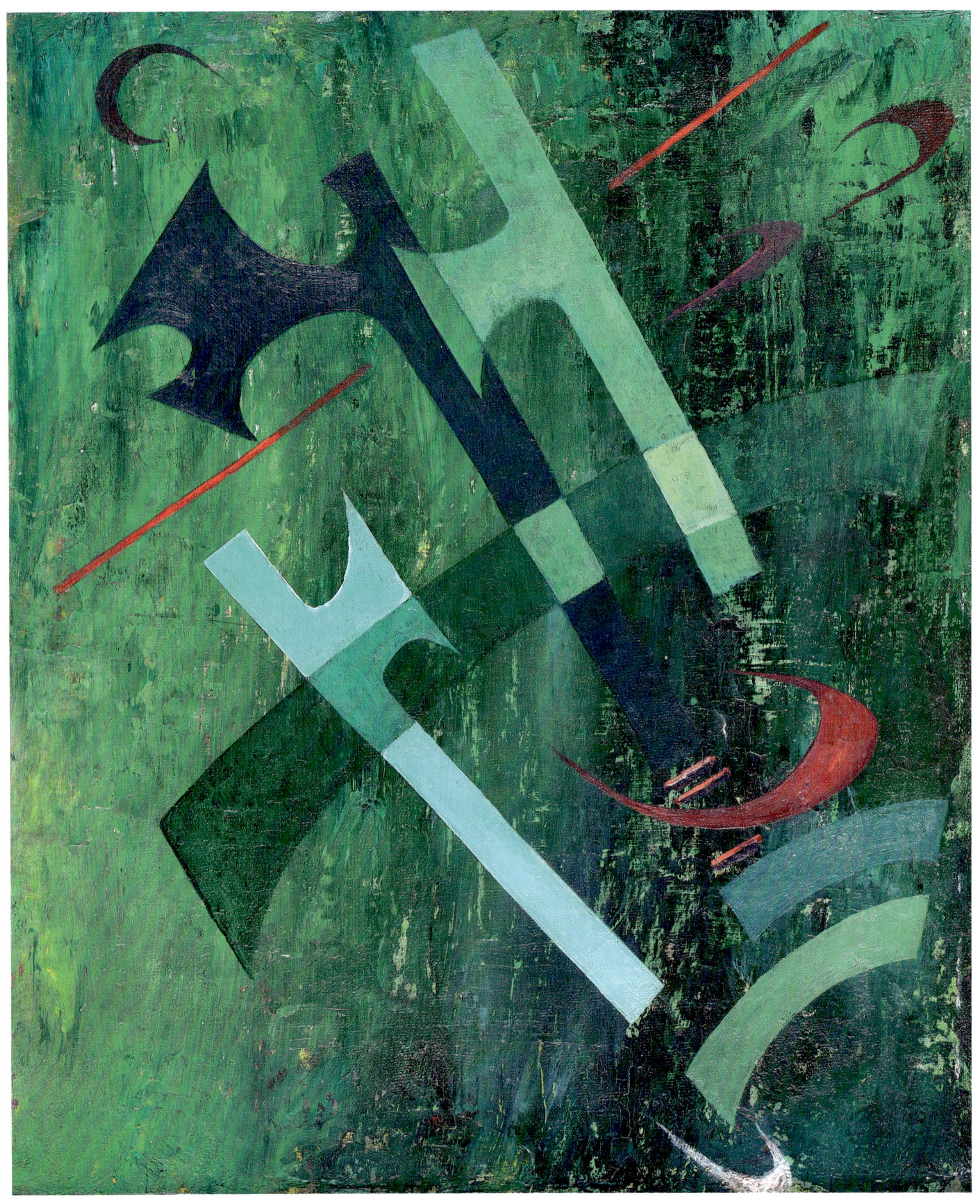

"GREEN ORGANIZATION" 1943   36

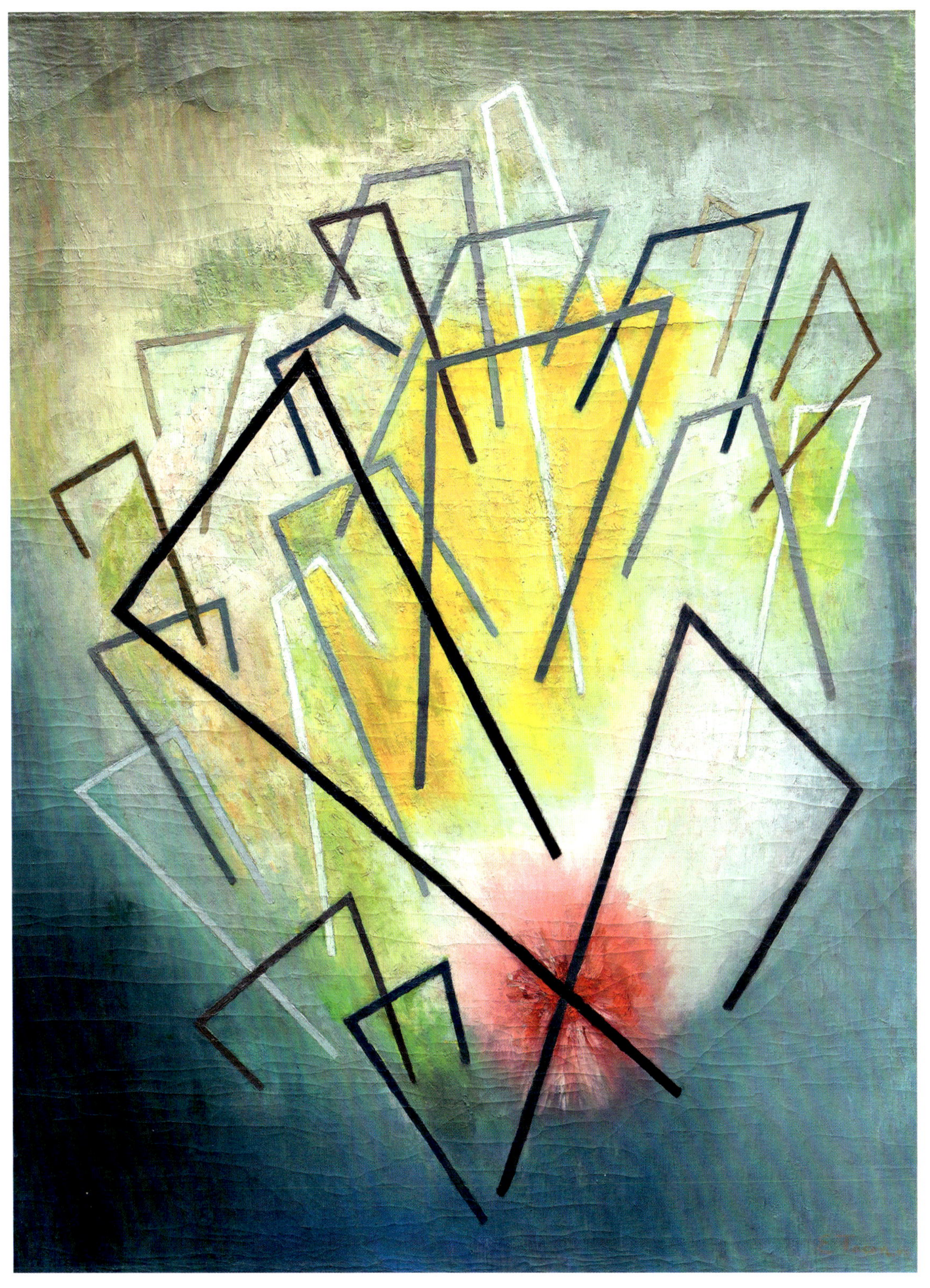

"UNTITLED ABSTRACTION" 1945

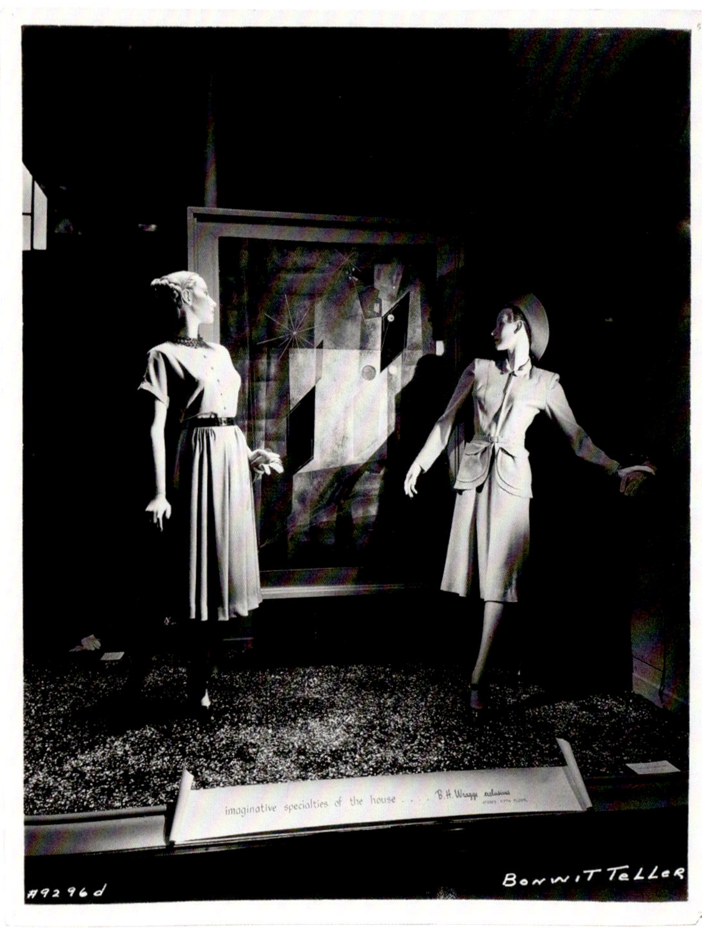

Bonwit Teller window display with artwork by Rolph Scarlett from the Museum of Non-Objective Painting, New York City, 1947

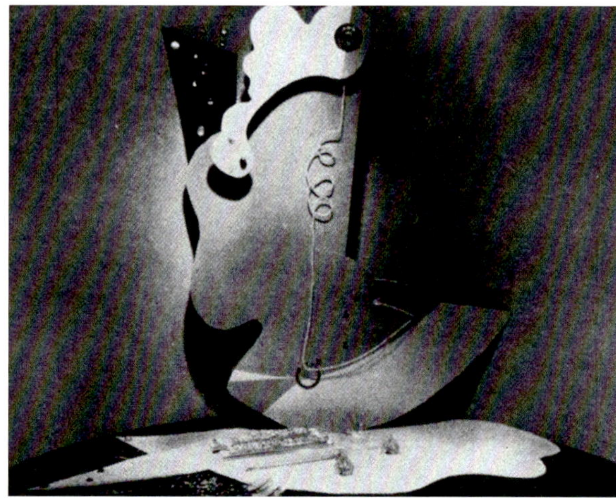

Diamond Christmas window display by Edna Taçon, December 1941

43. Letter from Taçon to Rebay, February 22, 1943.
Guggenheim Museum Archives, M0007-148-47.

44. Letter from Rebay to Taçon, December 7, 1943.
Guggenheim Museum Archives,
M0007-148-47.

45. Letter from Rebay to Taçon, November 19, 1942.
Guggenheim Museum Archives,
A0010-3034-1.

46. Zemans, *New Perspectives on Modernism in
Canada*, 30. This image is attributed to another
artist in *Fortune* magazine.

47. Despite Rebay's admonishment of Taçon's
window displays, six years later, in 1947,
the MNOP lent works from the collection
to Bonwit Teller, a New York department
store, for fashion displays and photoshoots,
thereby suggesting that non-objective
art was fashionable and of the moment (see
p. 38, top).

48. Isabel McLaughlin fonds at Queen's University,
1933–1942, 230337-2-13.

49. Email correspondence with Claire Taçon, the
artist's granddaughter, May 9, 2025.

50. Foster, "The Feminine Outlook."

I dislike having such a burden as these bills hanging over my head
but I have no way to solve the situation. All thru [*sic*] these trying weeks
I have not missed a day from the Museum and I believe that if I had
been isolated away from this environment I might have felt even worse.
There is no denying the Museum is a most inspiring place and I am
happy to be with the Foundation. We all miss your visits here and your
constructive help with our work.[43]

That December, Rebay wrote: "I shall see that you get full pay so as to help you
in difficult times, and to have a happy Christmas."[44] In a letter from the year prior,
Rebay wrote to Taçon:

Please write to me, also, about your own self and how your family is.
Be careful to avoid in your paintings the decorative effect and search
for the creative lasting singularity, otherwise, you will not improve.
Do not look for job [*sic*]; like window displays, as it will tarden [*sic*] your
progress in art. As you now have a steady job, you do not have to.[45]

Taçon's ability to create window displays, despite having been discouraged by
Rebay, would have been a much-needed source of independent income for
Taçon. Shop-window design was another remarkable aspect of her career that
illustrates her adaptability and the multifaceted nature of her artistic vision. Little
has been documented about her early design work, except for a window display
called *Diamond Christmas* that she made in December 1941 for a jeweller on
Fifth Avenue. The display, which was reproduced in *Fortune* magazine,[46] resembled
her collages in the way that the lyrical, biomorphic elements were dramatically
lit to define three-dimensional space in a decidedly modern shop window (p. 38).[47]
That year, Taçon made her own Christmas cards, illustrated with a black-and-white
photograph of *Diamond Christmas* and red collaged paper—a sign of how
proud she was of the window display.[48] Taçon's commercial work also included
a three-part mural for a restaurant (pp. 40–41). While its location and dates are
unknown, the mural's underwater scenes reveal a much more whimsical side to
Taçon's practice. Like her window display, here she engaged with architectural
space on a grand scale to create her largest-ever work.

The artist's interest in design extended to various other endeavours, including
dressmaking, millinery, and jewellery-making. This creative flexibility, and particularly her interest in fashion, may have been informed by her father, who worked
as both a tailor and musician. Her artistic spectrum was full, and she did not seek
to separate "fine art," fashion, craft, and life.[49] She even ran a gift shop out of her
Hamilton home, selling handmade objects like Christmas ornaments and paper-
weights.[50] She later designed plexiglass prisms, sometimes used on necklaces, that

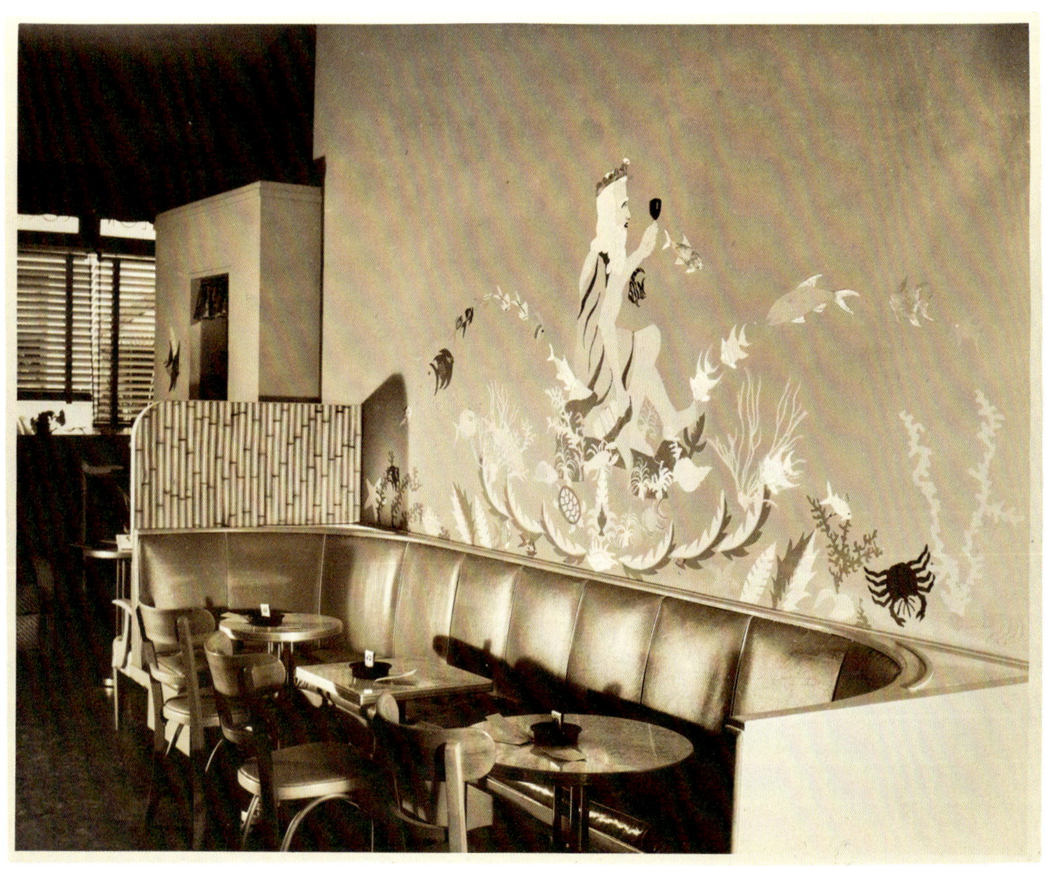
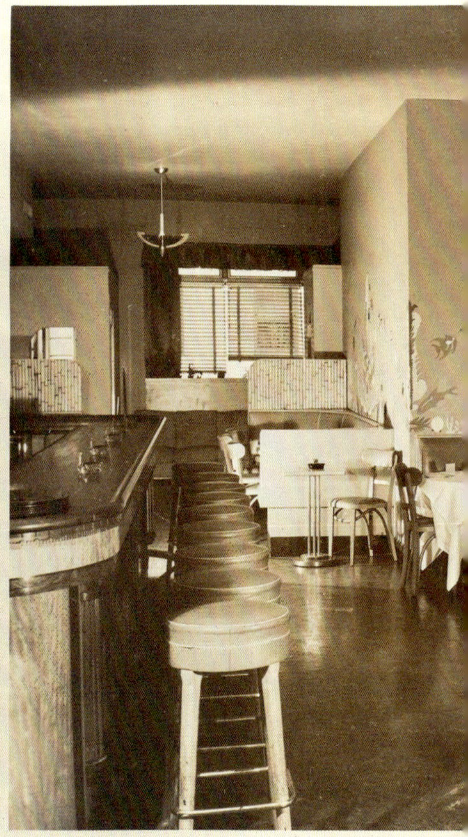

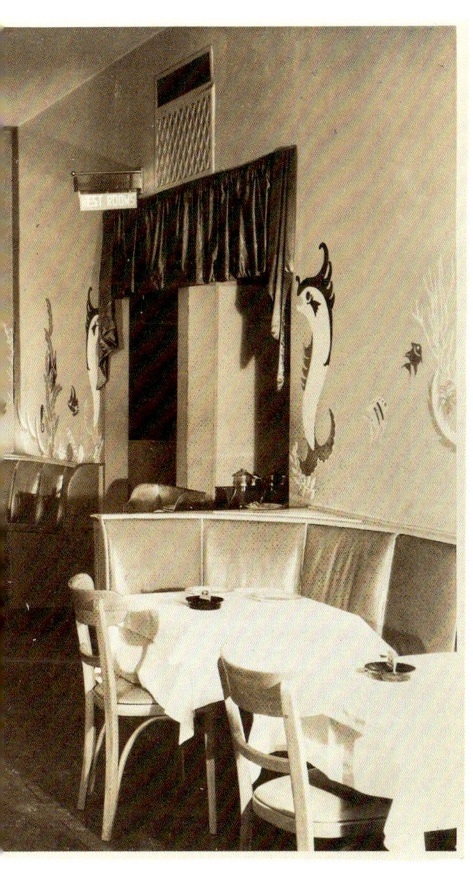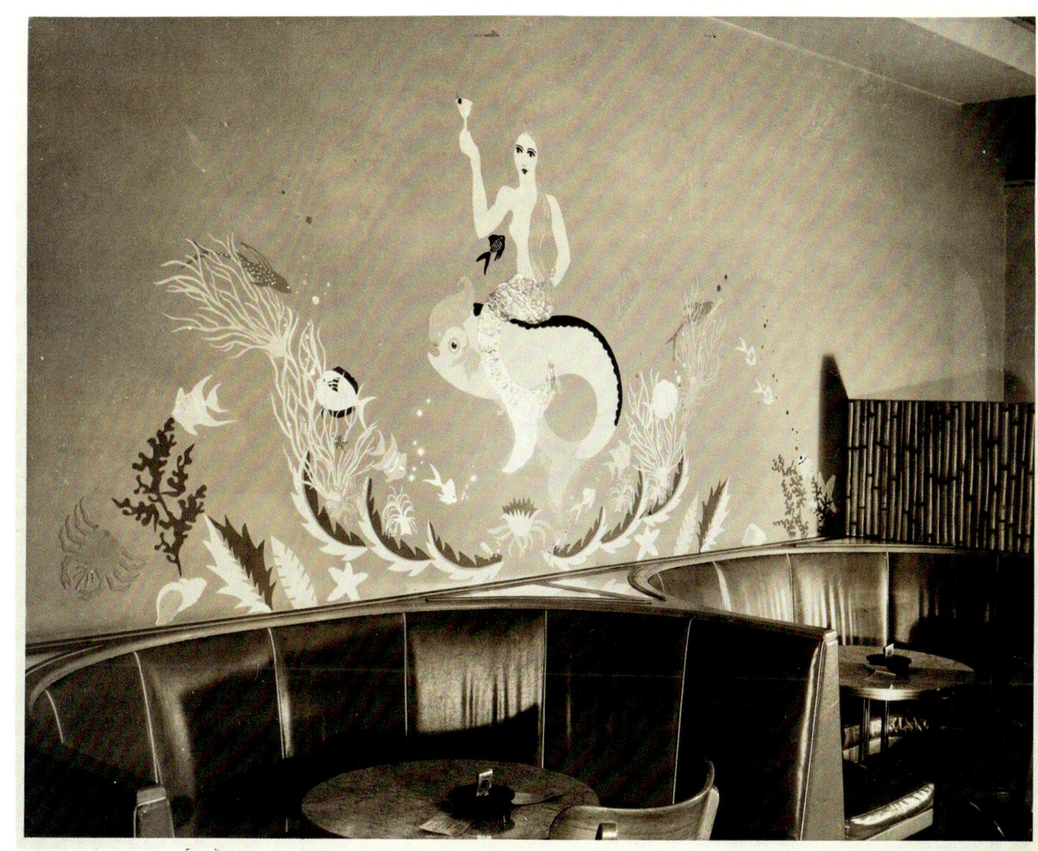

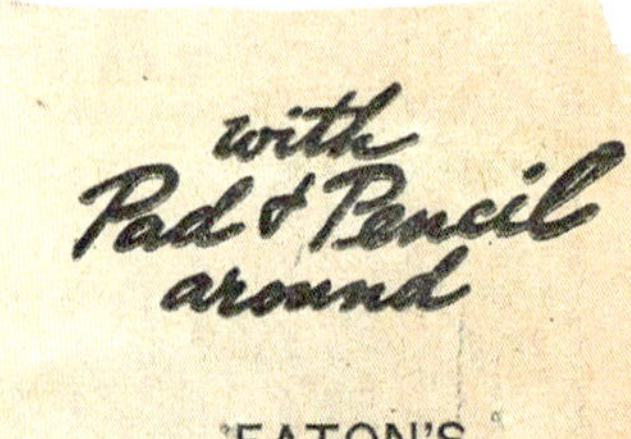

EATON'S
COLLEGE STREET,

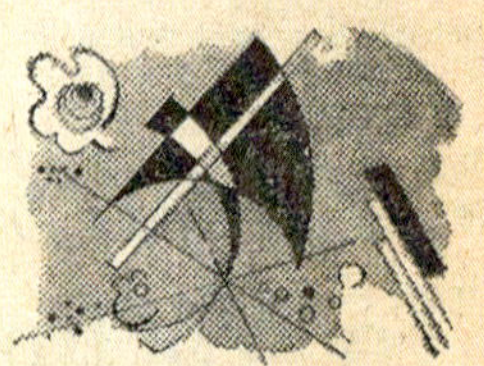

NON-OBJECTIVE
PAINTINGS—

Triangles, circles, squares
. . . vivid colours . . . such is
the newest style in artistic
form. Edna Tacon, a fore-
most exponent of this style
that uses neither landscapes
nor portraits, and yet arouses
aesthetic feeling, is exhibiting
her works for the third time
in Toronto. Her style is
highly controversial, but be
you pro or con, her exhibition
is not to be missed! Fine Art
Galleries—Second Floor.

were hand-painted and sold as "designs by Edna Taçon." The artist was also compelled to make her living space unique and beautiful by collecting ornate linens, and by making intricate textiles such as hand-beaded and embroidered Christmas stockings for her sons.[51]

Eaton's: Recent Experiments

Taçon's solo show at Eaton's Fine Art Galleries in November 1941 was the first exhibition dedicated to non-objective art in Canada. Unlike in New York, the cultural climate in 1940s Toronto was conservative, with few artists working outside the traditional genres of landscape and figuration. Taçon's exhibition was therefore deemed radical, and it received extensive media coverage. Pearl McCarthy described Taçon's collages as a kind of "transcendental technique" with pieces "hardly wider than a hair's breadth"[52] and later encouraged visitors to "look for design, colour sense and texture devised with infinite work as well as sparkle to rouse feelings."[53] McCarthy also reported that "lively comment rises in the gallery.... Artists are returning several times to the exhibit. P. H. Taçon is to speak on the pictures this afternoon."[54]

Other Toronto critics were positive but less enthusiastic about—and perhaps caught off guard by—Taçon's first show at Eaton's.[55] In the *Canadian Review*, her works were considered to range widely in merit from "over-complicated and life-less" to "singularly complete and moving." The medium of collage was described as "unfamiliar to most Canadians."[56] Another reviewer praised Taçon's "delightful conjunctions of colour and...the curiously crisp designs...even though it is strictly necessary to consult the catalogue as to what the artist had in mind."[57] Non-objective art was clearly at odds with the conventional trends in Toronto at the time.

The following year, 1942, proved equally productive for Taçon, who showed work in three more group exhibitions at the MNOP; another at the Women's Art Association of Hamilton's 46th annual exhibition, where hers were the only abstract works included; and in a second solo show at Eaton's titled *Exhibition of Recent Experiments in Non-Objective Art by Edna Taçon*. These "recent experiments" included oil paintings on vellum, paper plastics, and watercolours.[58] Around this time, Taçon moved away from precise geometric forms toward a more ethereal type of abstraction. She began to employ expressive lines with the added effect of sprayed or stippled paint on the surfaces. This experimentation caused some controversy among critics: "Several of the tempera paintings show evidence of paint applied with an atomizer, which in my humble opinion, violates one of the basic conans [*sic*] of art."[59] As in her earlier collages, here Taçon's fine linework adds an aura of elegance and delicateness.

Eaton's Fine Art Galleries played an important role both in the development of Taçon's career and Canadian abstract art in the 1940s more broadly.

51. Email correspondence with Claire Taçon, May 9, 2025.

52. Pearl McCarthy, "Art and Artists," *The Globe and Mail* (August 2, 1941).

53. McCarthy, "Art and Artists," November 1, 1941.

54. This is the only instance on record that Percy spoke publicly about Edna's artwork. It signals that he was involved and had some sense of expertise or authority on the subject matter and Edna's work. In later years, she would speak publicly about her own work.

55. Taçon's sales records from Eaton's are unknown.

56. "Reviews: Eaton's Galleries," *Canadian Review* (November 1941), signed "C.W."

57. "Non-Objective Paintings in Paper Plastic Form," *The Evening Telegram* (November 1941).

58. Three untitled works on paper (see pp. 20, 21, and 23) are indicative of the style in which she was working in 1940–42. It is unconfirmed whether these three were included in *Exhibition of Recent Experiments in Non-Objective Art by Edna Taçon* at Eaton's.

59. Brock Brace, "Aucun a sa Façon / Eaton's Galleries," *The Varsity* (November 1942).

Eaton's fall exhibitions announcement, 1944

IT'S REALLY WORTH WHILE TO VISIT
The Fine Art Galleries
AT EATON'S-COLLEGE STREET

These galleries play a double roll . . . not only presenting a complete range of paintings for every taste . . . but also presenting from time to time exhibitions by gifted artists which because of their stimulating character should point the way to more complete enjoyment of the visual arts.

To illustrate this double roll, we list below some of the exhibitions to be shown this fall.

- "Three Painters from Ottawa" — A. Burton, R. Gravel and T. Wood.
- Non-Objective Paintings — by Edna Taçon.
- "Adventure in Art" — paintings by 20 of Canada's outstanding modernists.
- Marc Aurèle Fortin — celebrated Montreal Painter.
- Flower Paintings — Estelle Kerr, Helen McClain and Beatrice Robertson.
- Frederick H. Varley — comprehensive one man show.
- Seascapes — by Jaffrey Harris — California Painter.
- Tom Stone — Annual Exhibition.
- Water Colours — by Peggy Brisby.
- Herbert Palmer — Annual Exhibition.

—SECOND FLOOR

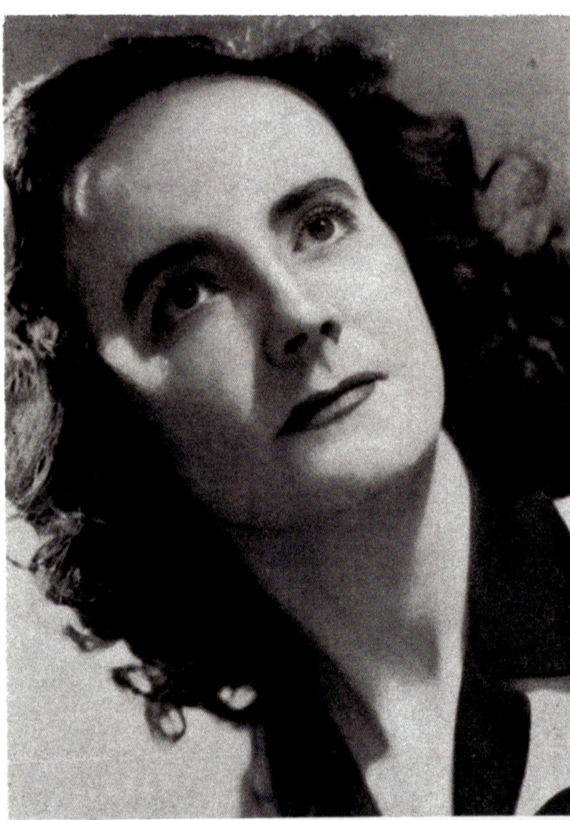

EXPONENT OF
NON-OBJECTIVE
PAINTING

EDNA • TAÇON •

COMPOSITION
ON PINK
(oil on parchment)
SIZE: 19″ x 24″

Private Collection of Solomon Guggenheim, New York City.

Thought may be grave or gay, but always there must be power for its control and dynamic energy to make it avail. In this discipline, as expressed in "Composition on Pink," a slender bright line, alive as a whip lash, can hold together a piercing black shaft of an idea and triangles of sharp intensity. It is civilized force, rich, alive.

E. T.

Exhibition pamphlet for *Edna Taçon: Exponent of Non-Objective Painting,* Eaton's Fine Art Galleries, 1944

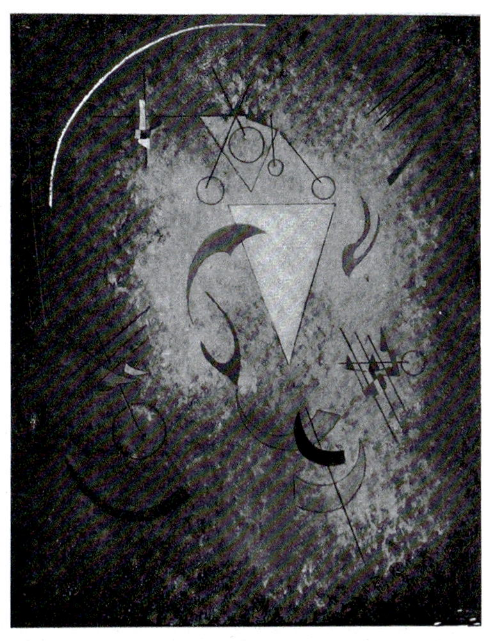

SUFFICIENCY

(watercolour)
SIZE: 19" x 24"

For every man who is capable of finding himself in the solitude of his mind, there is one hour which is prized above all. It comes when, in contemplation, the divergent shapes of his ideals are brought into harmony. Then he may know the white ecstacy of mental efforts fulfilled. Such luminous moment is expressed in "Sufficiency."

E. T.

Comments On Non-Objective Paintings.

THESE PAMPHLETS CONTAIN EXTRACTS FROM THE WRITINGS OF HILLA REBAY, CURATOR OF THE GUGGENHEIM FOUNDATION, NEW YORK CITY.

In order to make full presentation of the non-objectivists' attitude we have refrained from censoring questionable points of view.

THESE PAMPHLETS ARE PRESENTED, THEN, AS REPRESENTING THE PERSONAL OPINIONS OF HILLA REBAY.

IF YOU ARE INTERESTED, PLEASE FEEL FREE TO TAKE ONE.

Comments on Non-Objective Paintings, Eaton's Fine Art Galleries exhibition pamphlet, c. 1946

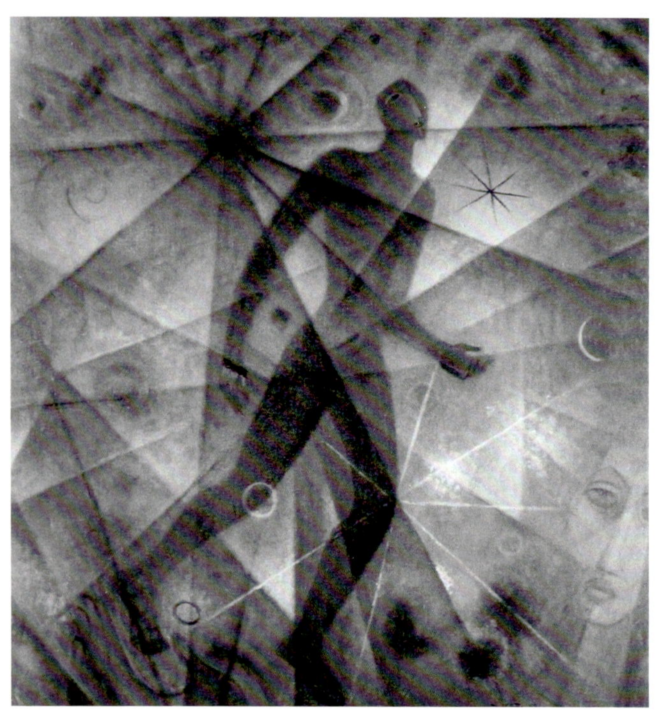

Marian Dale Scott, *Variations on
a Theme—Cell and Fossil*, 1946

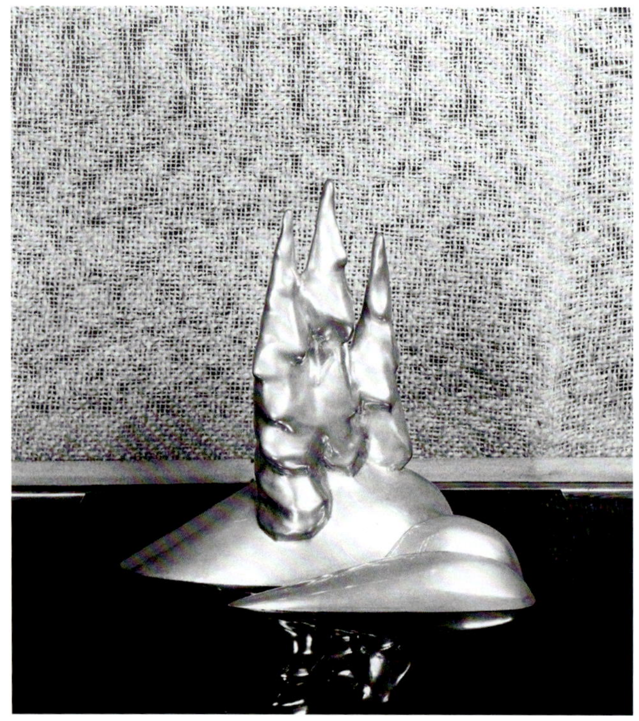

Elizabeth Wyn Wood, *Cedar*, c. 1930–40

60. Paul Duval, "Art in the Department
Store," *Canadian Art*, vol. 11, no. 3
(March 1945): 126.

61. Zemans, *New Perspectives on
Modernism in Canada*, 34.

62. Taçon quoted in Kenneth Dawson,
"The Art of Edna Taçon,"
Canadian Review of Music and Art
vol. 3, nos. 7–8 (1944): 24.

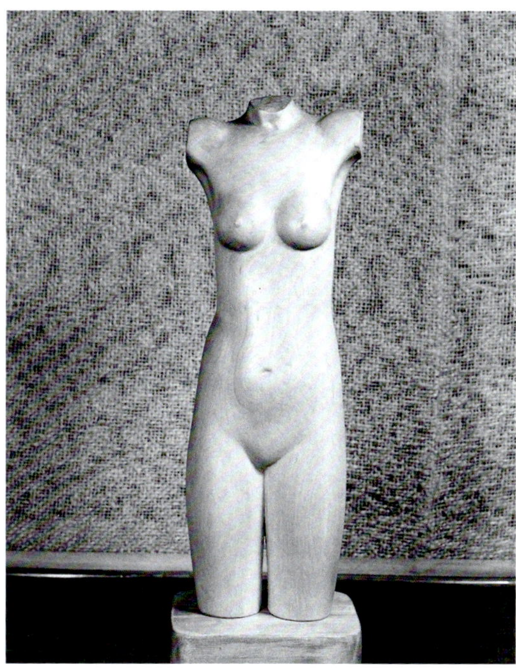

Occupying four rooms and a large rotunda within Eaton's department store on College Street in Toronto, the galleries displayed artwork ranging from traditional paintings that would be commercially successful to "radical" Canadian art by emerging artists, such as Taçon and other progressive artists like Marian Dale Scott (1906–1933) (p. 46, top), Elizabeth Wyn Wood (1903–1966) (p. 46, bottom), and Florence Wyle (1881–1968) (left). Art writer Paul Duval described Eaton's as a space that was "equal in lighting and general layout to any of the 57th Street art salons of New York."[60] The galleries attracted high attendance numbers using newspaper ads and direct-mail announcements of exhibitions. Eaton's also scouted new talent and encouraged artists who took risks, Duval noted, "introducing countless citizens of Toronto and visitors to the most recent developments in Canadian art."

In addition, Eaton's served an educational purpose by inviting artists to give talks about their work and display written statements in their exhibitions. These interpretive strategies enabled Taçon to share her philosophies (as well as those of Kandinsky and the MNOP) and help visitors understand her artwork and non-objective painting as a genre. The Eaton's Galleries archives contain a hand-painted sign that was likely included in Taçon's 1946 solo exhibition, advertising pamphlets of Hilla Rebay's writings on non-objectivity (p. 45).

In 1942 and 1943, while exhibiting at Eaton's, Taçon was still working for months at a time at the MNOP in New York. As the Guggenheim Foundation's spokesperson in Canada, she remained dedicated to promoting modernism and a greater understanding of non-objectivity and abstraction. In 1943, Rebay wrote of her: "She is still a *very* fine artist and one who represents us and helps us so much in Canada."[61]

Ever-Evolving Style

"Vibrant blues and greens, unexpected devices of design dash into a bright rhythm. A certain grandeur or dignity is seen in their concerted brilliance. Verve and decorum combine."—Edna Taçon[62]

By 1943, Taçon's reputation as a leading contemporary artist in Toronto had crystallized. Her relationship with the Art Gallery of Toronto began in May of that year with the exhibition *Four Canadian Artists: Jessie Faunt, Michael Forster, Edna Taçon, Gordon Webber*. As the only non-objective artist, Taçon exhibited fifteen pieces—including *Composition on Pink* (p. 50)—alongside works by similarly emerging, experimental artists.

A study of the intersection between space and time, the work is a balanced and precise composition that exemplifies a shift in Taçon's style; she had become more experimental with materials, and her work conveyed greater sophistication

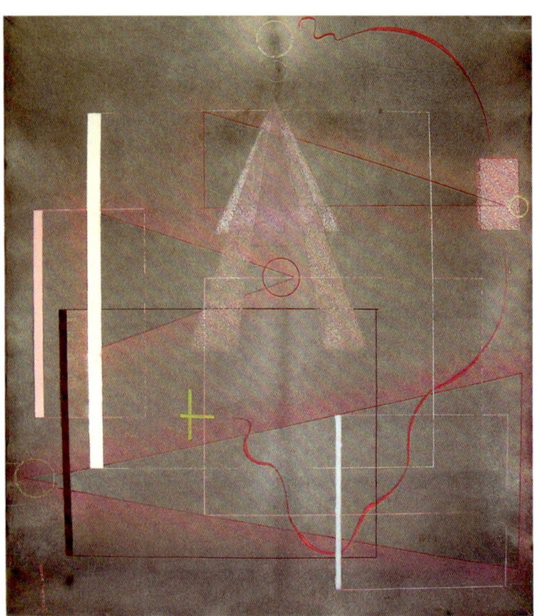

Edna Taçon, *Composition*, 1942

that was more advanced compositionally. The suspended arrangement of geometric forms on vellum shows the artist's remarkable ability to bring divergent shapes—swirling circles and triangles—and sinuous lines into rhythmic harmony. Taçon writes: "In *Composition on Pink*, a slender bright line, alive as a whiplash, can hold together a piercing black shaft of an idea and triangles of sharp intensity."[63] Pearl McCarthy reported on the texture achieved in some of Taçon's works from this time: "A few painters have been experimenting assiduously in the use of parchment, or skins, discovering new fare for the senses in the colours and textures they obtain."[64]

In 1942 and 1943, Taçon produced several other works on vellum.[65] Other artists such as John Sennhauser (1907–1978), who participated in MNOP group exhibitions, also made paintings on vellum. Indeed, the material—natural animal skin historically used for illuminated manuscripts—enhanced colours and the impression of objects floating in space. The use of vellum by Taçon and others is attributable to the exchange and collaboration among artists associated with the MNOP.[66] By their nature, paintings on vellum are highly sensitive to moisture and environmental changes. Two extant paintings on vellum by Taçon were acquired by the MNOP—*Twist* (1942) and *Composition* (1942; left), now held in the Solomon R. Guggenheim Founding Collection—along with *Composition on Pink*, also on vellum.[67]

Installation photography from Taçon's third solo exhibition at Eaton's in January 1944 reveals that she had embraced the interior design of the MNOP (pp. 52–53). She created a meditative setting by covering walls with pleated velour fabric and paintings hung low to the room's wainscotting. The works, available for purchase at $1,000 CAD each,[68] characteristically referenced music in their titles, including *Fugue* and *Sonata* (dates unknown). Taçon prepared pamphlets for this "highly controversial"[69] exhibition, and—as at the MNOP, where docents were encouraged to speak with visitors to reduce the formality of the space—Taçon made herself available to engage with the public during the run of this show. Eaton's harnessed the debate around non-objective art as a provocative marketing tool, exclaiming that "be you pro or con, her [Taçon's] exhibition is not to be missed!"[70] McCarthy lauded this exhibition as "the very best she has presented."[71]

There is little of Taçon's own writing available from 1944, and even fewer details about her personal life; however, McCarthy continued to review her work often, assiduously noting that Taçon's practice had evolved further. She transitioned from the precise, solid geometric shapes of her paper plastics to a more expressive painterliness, with glowing forms rendered through a loose blending of colours. In reference to a watercolour titled *Caprice* (1944), the artist notes that "dark philosophical hues are banished. Pinks and violets are liberated for a carefree celebration, and the oval forms are simple enough to make the composition bespeak a holiday from anxiety."[72] A canvas also titled *Caprice* (p. 54)

63. Taçon quoted in Dawson, "The Art of Edna Taçon," 22.

64. Pearl McCarthy, "Canadian's Work Bought in U.S.A." *The Globe and Mail* (March 1943).

65. The vellum she used during this time was prepared by George A. Hathaway, who may have been an artist or employee at the MNOP. Karole Vail, *The Museum of Non-Objective Painting: Hilla Rebay and the Origins of the Solomon R. Guggenheim Museum* (The Guggenheim Museum, 2009), 270.

66. Zemans, *New Perspectives on Modernism in Canada*, 32.

67. In 2025, the Solomon R. Guggenheim Museum accessioned two additional works by Edna Taçon: *Untitled* (p. 35) and *Swinging* (p. 51).

68. Bridle, "Look at a Fugue and Take it Home."

69. "With Pad + Pencil Around, Non-Objective Paintings," Eaton's Fine Art Galleries, January 1944.

70. Ibid.

71. Pearl McCarthy, "Art and Artists: Plan Challenges Citizens' Energy," *The Globe and Mail* (January 8, 1944).

72. "Edna Taçon: Exponent on Non-Objective Painting," Eaton's Fine Art Galleries, September 1944.

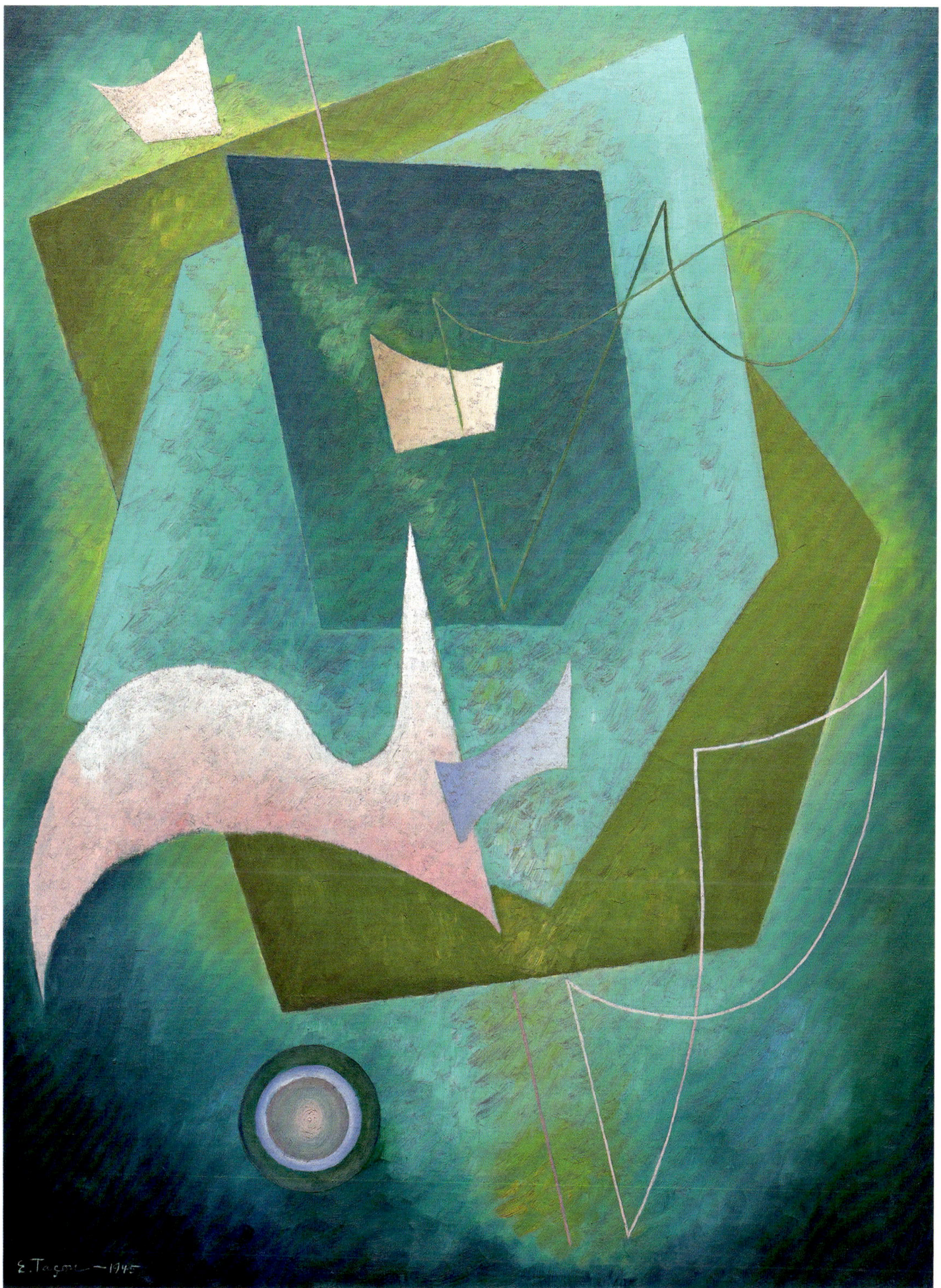

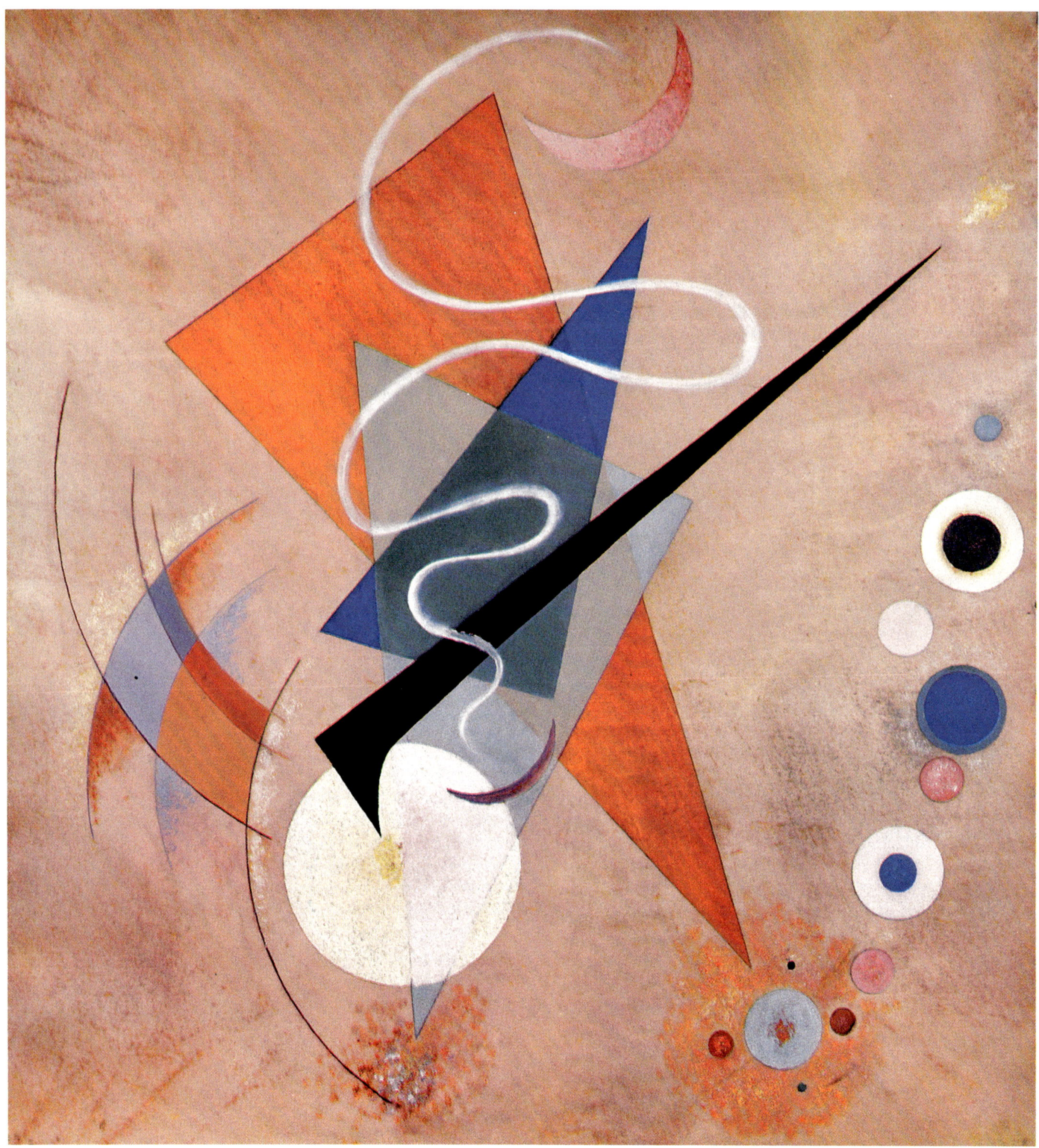

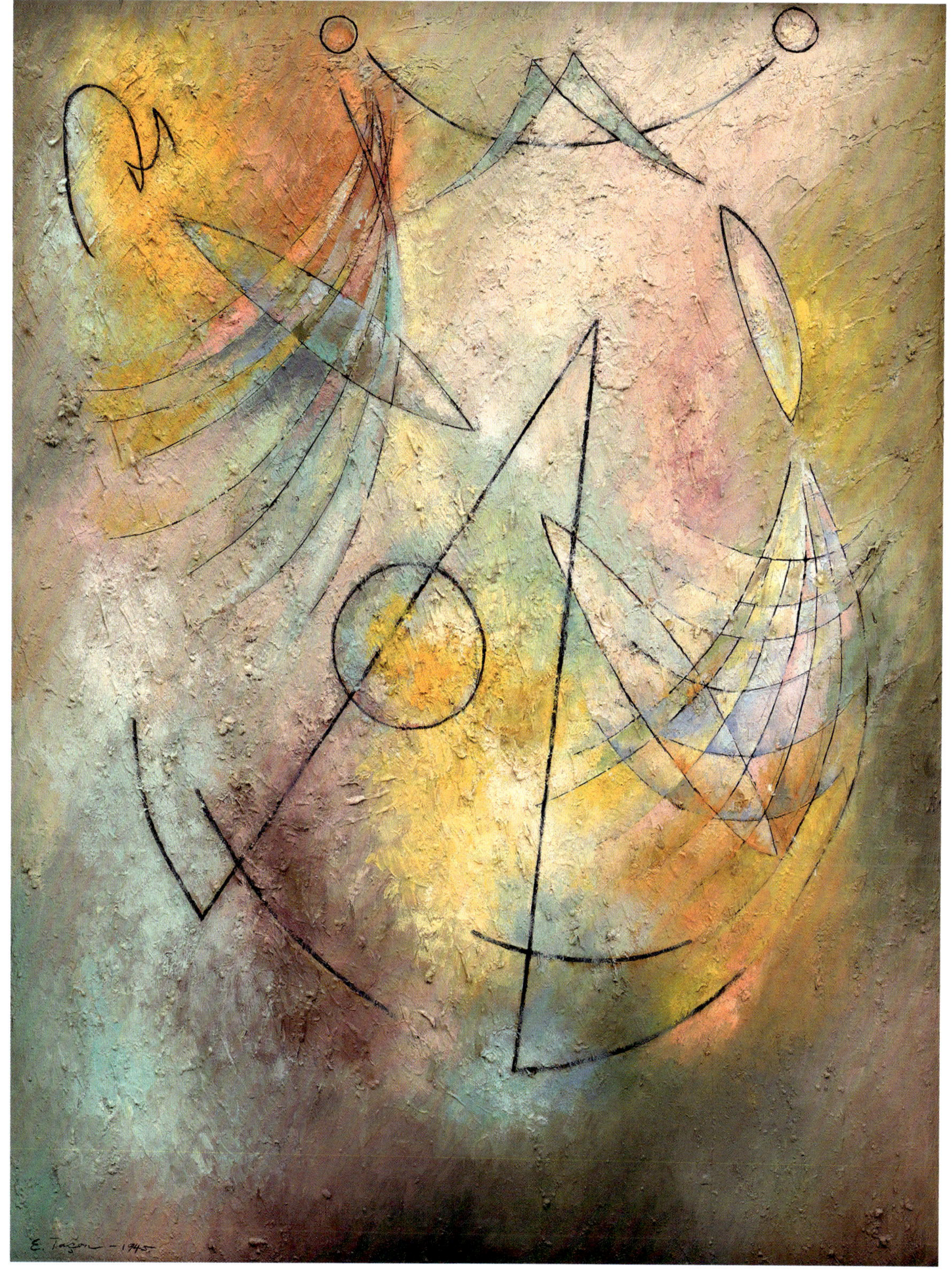

"SWINGING" 1945

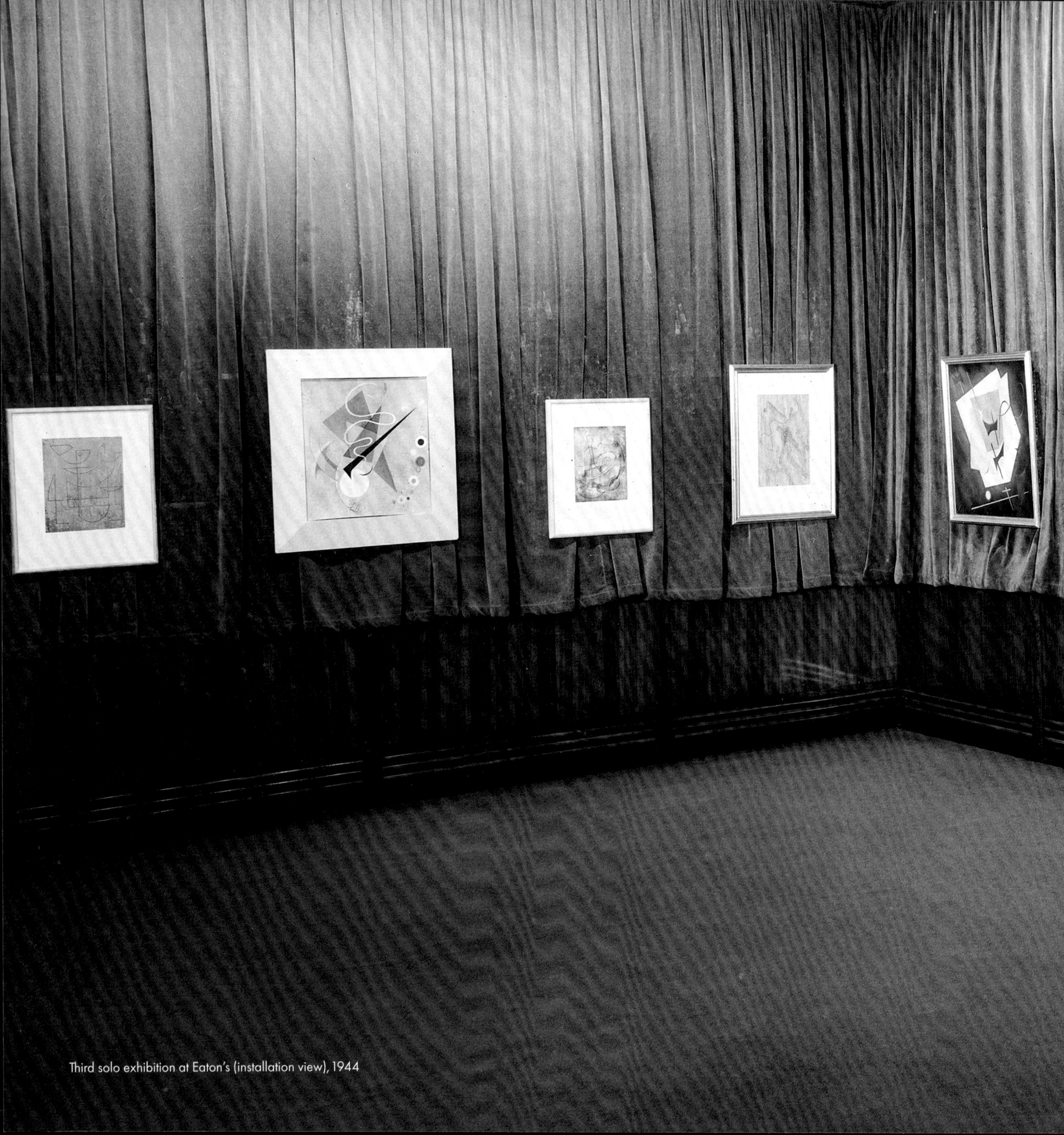

Third solo exhibition at Eaton's (installation view), 1944

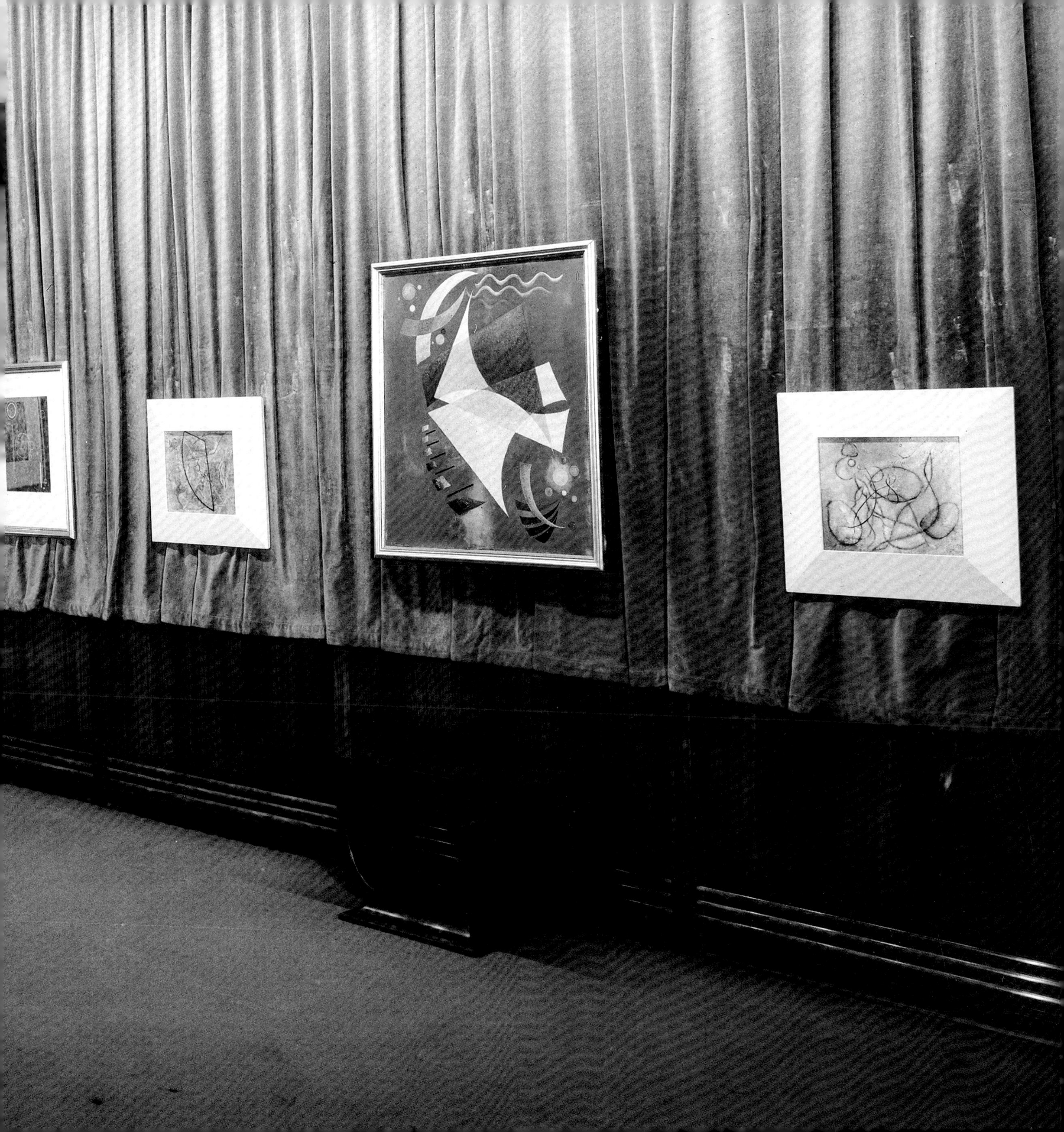

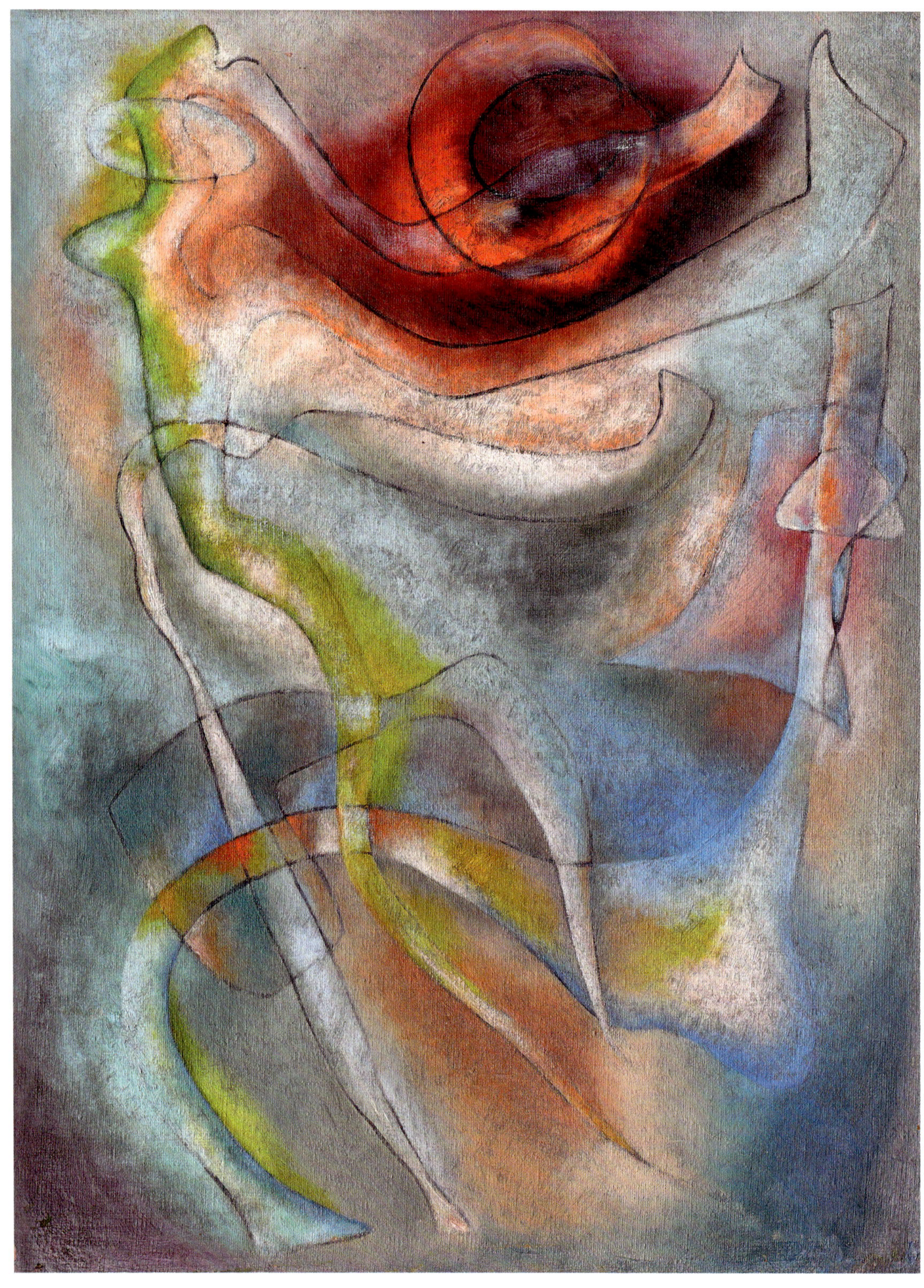

"CAPRICE" c. 1946

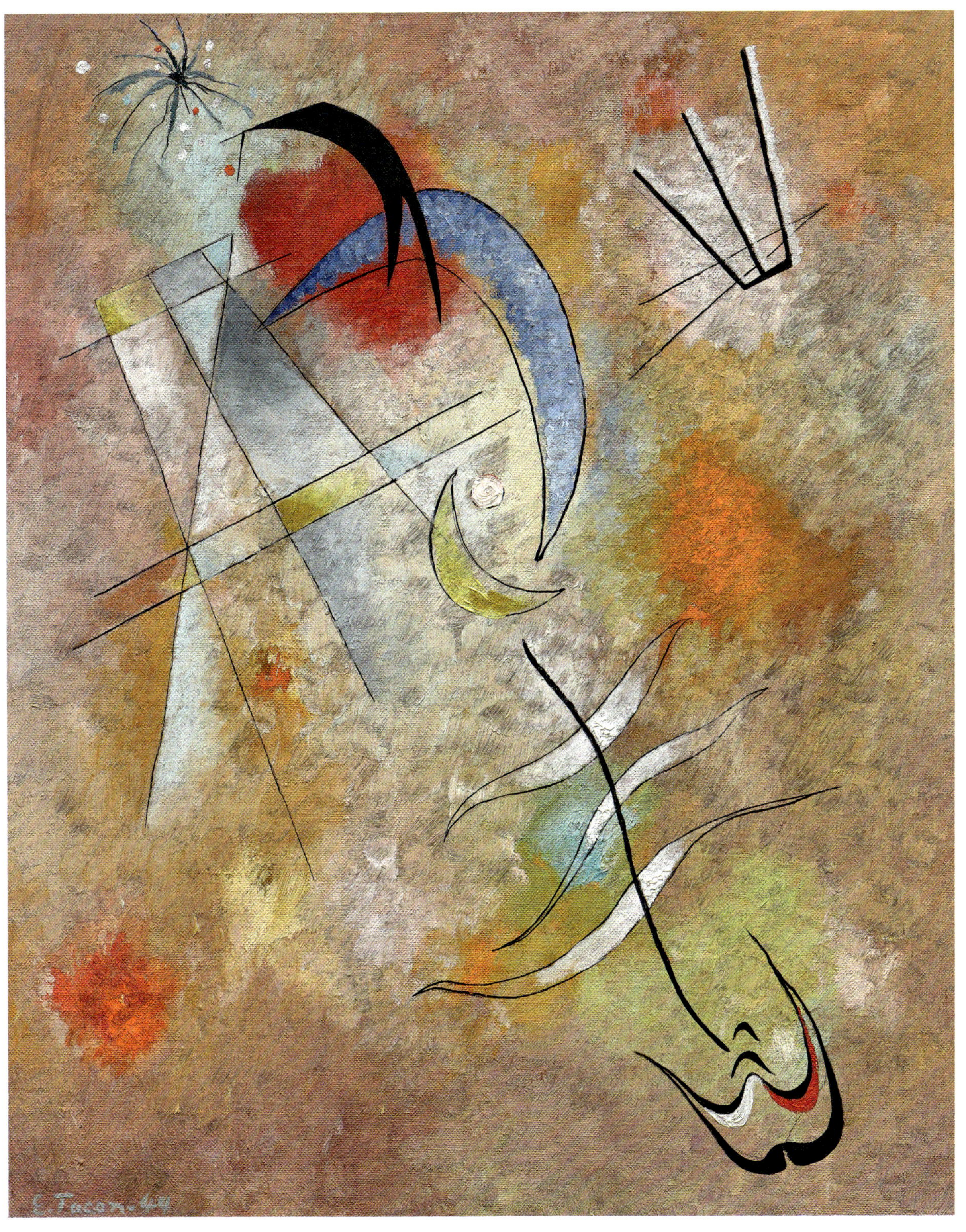

55

"ECSTASY (BLACK ACCENT)" 1944

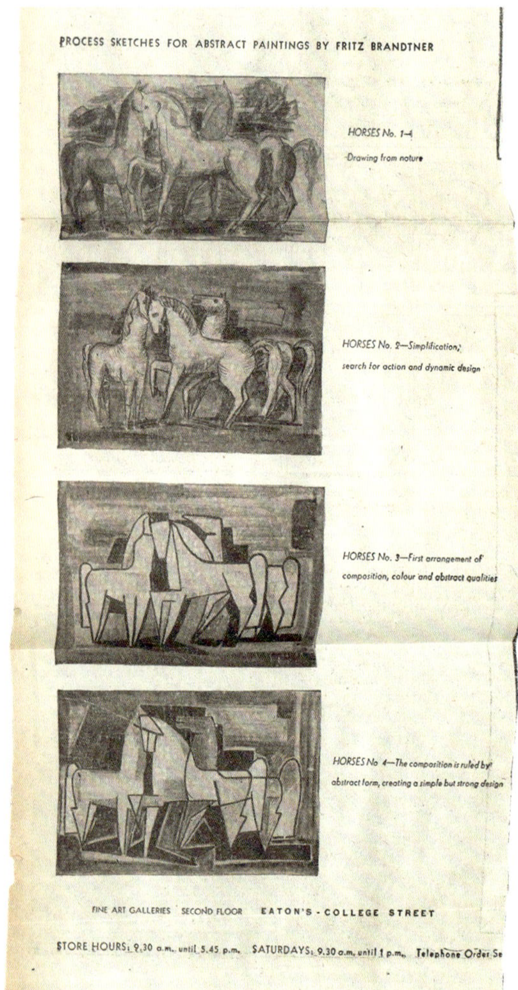

Eaton's ad for *Excursion in Abstract* with drawings by
Fritz Brandtner, January 27, 1945

exemplifies similar stylistic decisions. Lyrical lines evoke movement and biomorphic energy with a gradient colouration that suggests depth, while the background is richly worked, enhanced by whiteish pinks, blues, and yellows to create a pastel-like quality.[73] She also used a dry brush to spread watercolour in thin layers and achieve a luminous effect. Notably, the title may hint at Taçon's emotional state while executing these works, and McCarthy once noted Taçon's "talent for creating a picture of emotion."[74]

Like Taçon's previous solo exhibition, the 1945 show *Excursion in Abstract* at Eaton's was meant to be educational. Curated by the contemporary abstract painters Fritz Brandtner (1896–1969), Henry Eveleigh (1909–1999), and Gordon Webber (1909–1965), this exhibition directly compared abstraction (Harris) with non-objectivity (Taçon). An ad in the *Toronto Star* stated that the curators' "accompanying comments and explanations form[ed] an integral part of the show"[75] and that they intended for the exhibition to "be a key to the layman's appreciation of abstract art...past and present."[76] Another ad included a suite of drawings by Brandtner that depicted a reverse step-by-step evolution: from a realistic drawing of horses to an increasingly simplified design to a final composition "ruled by abstract form."[77] This didactic tone would have been familiar to Taçon from her time as a docent at the MNOP as well as during the lectures she gave in Ontario and the United States to educate audiences about non-objectivity. With *Excursion in Abstract*, the fact that Taçon's work was selected by three progressive painters to be exhibited in a two-person show with Group of Seven co-founder Lawren Harris speaks to her prominence in Canadian art, in addition to her strong ties to a community of abstract artists dedicated to promoting their radical way of working.

Art Gallery of Toronto: Revelations

After *Excursion in Abstract*, Taçon continued to exhibit in prominent shows, maintaining her reputation as a leading artist in Toronto. In 1945, she exhibited at the Art Gallery of Toronto three times, first as part of an expansive touring exhibition called *The Development of Painting in Canada*. This survey, spanning from 1665 to 1945, included four abstract paintings by Lawren Harris, Marian Dale Scott, Gordon Webber, and Edna Taçon. These artists represented an aspect of contemporary painting described in the catalogue as "abstract or purely subjective painting in which no attempt is made to represent objects in the outside world."[78] With this exhibition—which travelled to the Art Association of Montreal, the National Gallery of Canada in Ottawa, and the Musée de la province de Québec (now the Musée national des beaux-arts du Québec) in Quebec City— Taçon was positioned as a forerunner of the latest trend in Canadian painting on a national scale.

73. In 1947, the AGT's acquisitions committee, with members including J.S. McLean, A.Y. Jackson, A.J. Casson, and Isabel McLaughlin, considered *Caprice* for the Gallery's collection; however, they decided to purchase another painting by Taçon called *Improvisation No. 2* (see p. 25).

74. McCarthy, "Emotions Are Pictured in Non-Objective Art."

75. "The Fine Arts Galleries Present: Excursion in Abstract," *Toronto Star* (January 31, 1945).

76. Ibid.

77. "Eaton's Fine Art Galleries Present Excursion in Abstract" advertisement, *The Globe and Mail* (January 27, 1945).

78. *The Development of Painting in Canada: 1665–1945* (Ryerson Press, 1945), 39.

79. *Ontario Society of Artists 73rd Annual Spring Exhibition*, Art Gallery of Toronto, March 3– April 1, 1945. The locations of these and many other Taçon works are unknown; they were likely sold to private collectors in Toronto and New York during the artist's lifetime.

80. "New Spirit, New Names Appear in Canadian Art," *The Evening Telegram* (March 3, 1945).

81. *Canadian Group of Painters* exhibition (Art Gallery of Toronto, Art Association of Montreal, 1946).

82. Graham McInnes, "Canadian Group of Painters," *Canadian Art*, vol. 3, no. 2 (1946): 76–77.

83. The inclusion of these artists who embraced modernism shows the openness of the CGP at the time.

The second AGT exhibition was with the Ontario Society of Artists (OSA), who invited Taçon to show two large paintings: *Lyrical Composition* and *Dynamic Organization* (dates unknown).[79] The exhibition was emblematic of a fresh, new spirit in Canadian art. *The Evening Telegram* commented on the significance of the avant-garde work on view and mentioned Taçon: "The octagonal room is set aside for experimental work…the interest lies in the curious revelations made—artists doing non-objective work."[80] Taçon would again show with the OSA during the next two years.

In her third appearance at the AGT in 1945, she was invited to exhibit with the Canadian Group of Painters (CGP)—a collective to which she would be elected a member in January 1946, thereby cementing her official acceptance into the Canadian art establishment.[81] *Tonal Poem* (p. 58) was illustrated in the exhibition brochure and described as well-painted and original, with "bold emotional simplicity."[82] It was installed in a room of abstract paintings, with work by artists including Marian Dale Scott, Lawren Harris, and Bertram Brooker.[83] *Tonal Poem*, like *Swinging* (p. 51), turns away from the hard-edge geometry of her earlier paper plastics and paintings on paper. With flowing forms drawn free-hand against a background of gradating patches of turquoise, red, cobalt, and grey punctuated by a gestural black linear form, the work is vaguely reminiscent of both a bass and treble clef, or perhaps the two combined.

In addition to the three AGT exhibitions, 1945 also marked Taçon's fifth solo show at Eaton's, where her signature non-objective style reached its apex. "This work is her very own, and, though the statement may seem very rash, the best

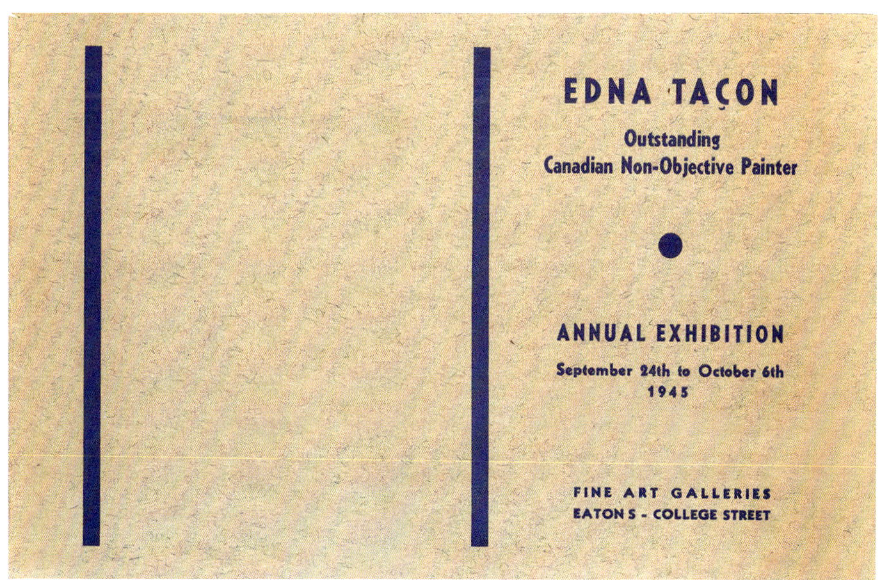

Exhibition pamphlet for *Edna Taçon: Outstanding Canadian Non-Objective Painter*, Eaton's Fine Art Galleries, 1945

84. Pearl McCarthy, "Art and Artists: The Taçon Art Comes of Age," *The Globe and Mail* (September 1945).

85. Pearl McCarthy, "Art and Artists: Taçon Painting Attracts in N.Y.," *The Globe and Mail* (November 9, 1946).

86. Taçon, Notebook [No. 3], cited in Zemans, *New Perspectives on Modernism in Canada*, 38.

87. Dorothy Howarth, "Some Husbands Pick Wives' Hats, Others Just Pay and Ignore 'Em," *The Evening Telegram* (July 25, 1946).

of it has no peer in its kind anywhere,"wrote McCarthy.[84] In addition to exhibiting her work, Taçon was identified as the leading exponent of non-objective art for actively promoting the movement in lectures throughout southern Ontario and in Michigan. Her audiences were mostly women's groups.

Contextualism

In 1945, Percy Taçon accepted a job as head of the art department with the Ontario College of Education at the University of Toronto (now the Ontario Institute for Studies in Education), and the family moved from Hamilton to Toronto. Taçon left the MNOP around this time and began working as a substitute teacher of design at Toronto's Western Technical School. Although no longer playing concerts, music remained a central theme in her art, and by 1946 her paintings still reflected a musical aspect as strong as they always had; however, they became increasingly expressive and less geometric. Works like *Improvisation No. 2* (p. 25) and *Gaiety* (right) recall her ethereal paintings on paper from the early 1940s and show a singular, expressive style that unites divergent shapes, lines, and colour fields into rhythmic harmony. Taçon likened visual rhythms through space that appeal to the eye with aural rhythms in time that appeal to the ear. Rendered with a remarkable painterliness, the sinuous lines and richly worked backgrounds in these paintings are still concerned with the potential visuality of sound.

Another important year, 1946 marked Taçon's solo exhibition at Chinese Gallery on 57th Street in New York. McCarthy observed the newness of the works, the maturity of Taçon's latest style, and her "individual, poetic contribution" in the genre.[85] *Edna Taçon: Contextualist* featured twenty-two watercolours and oils, including *Fleeing* (p. 63), one of her most colour-saturated canvases. Unlike Taçon's previous non-objective works, these paintings serve as metaphors to express states of being, inspired by the contextualist theory of beauty that weaves the subjective and objective together into subtle yet complex emotional compositions. Here, Taçon begins a transition away from non-objective art into a style that is more about communicating moods, opening up the composition, and shifting to more organic imagery. Taçon wrote: "With all my paintings, there is something of symbolism, of fantasy, of mysticism which ties up with a spiritual quality but with all relating to nature and life recognizable or not."[86]

In 1946, a photographic portrait of Taçon along with three other women appeared on the front page of Toronto's *The Evening Telegram* under the headline "Some Husbands Pick Wives' Hats, Others Just Pay and Ignore 'Em." The article (p. 86) described Taçon as a "non-objective painter [who] designs her own hats, and her husband really likes them."[87] Her expression is serious: she is positioning herself as an artist. The other women, named only *Mrs.* and the last name of their husbands, smile and appear carefree. The difference in Taçon's

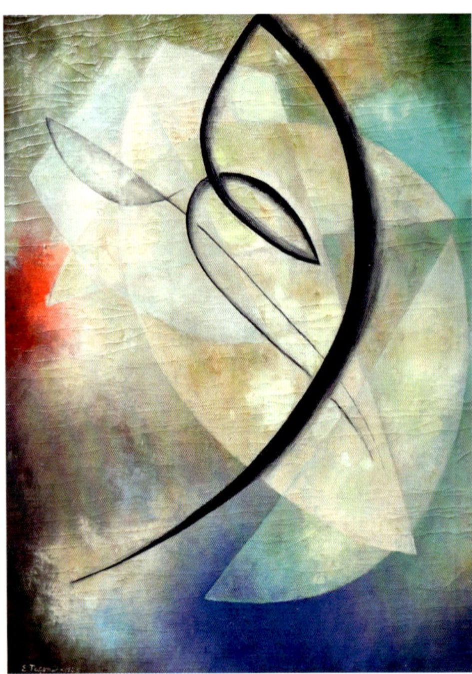

Edna Taçon, *Tonal Poem*, 1945

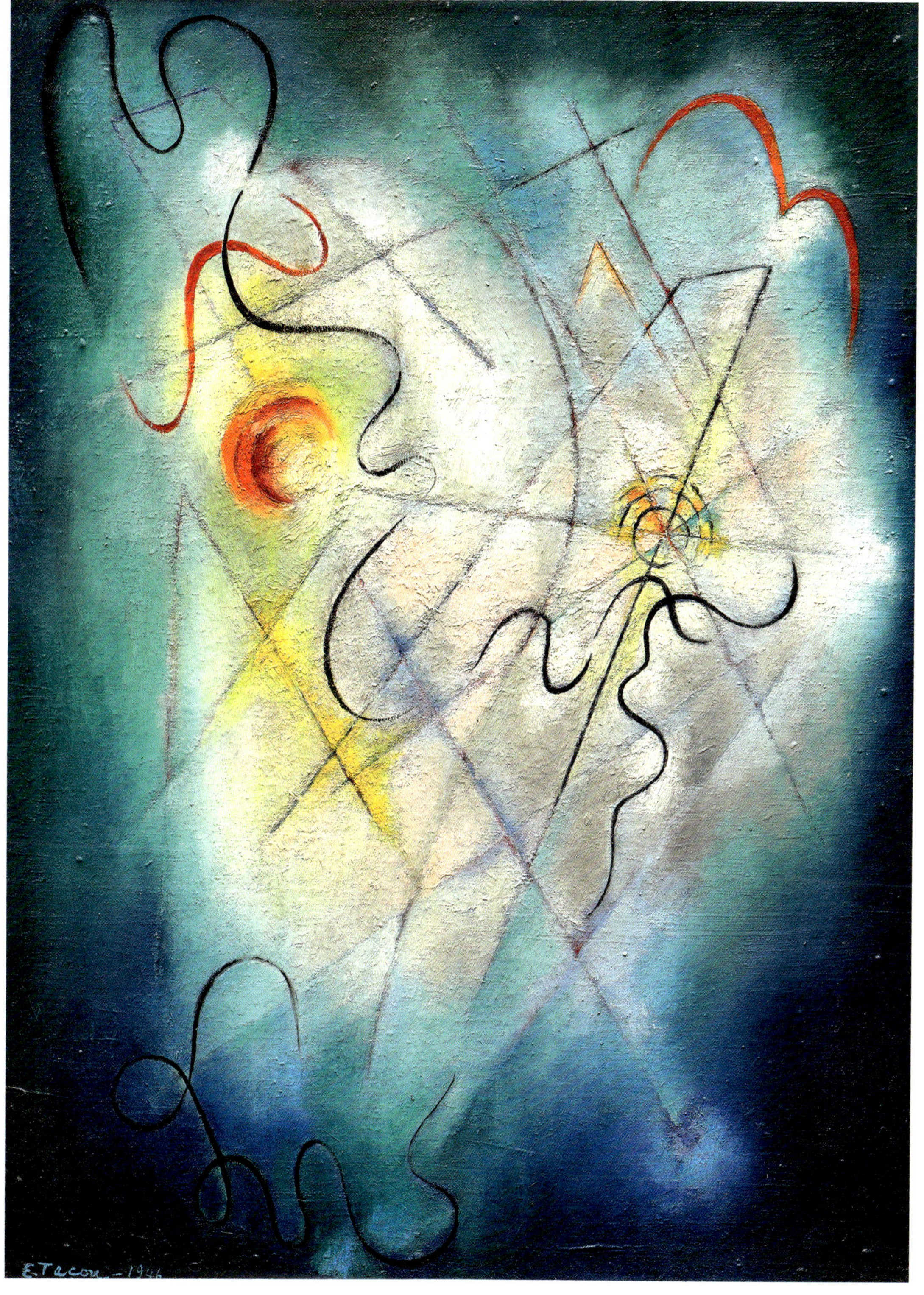

59

"GAIETY" 1946

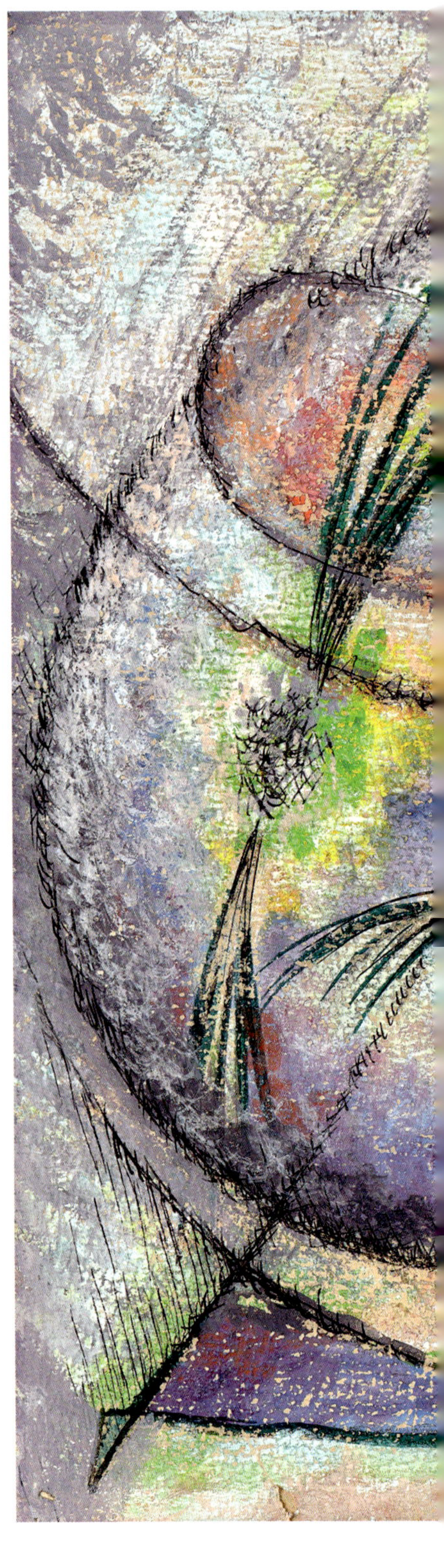

"ABSTRACT" 1948

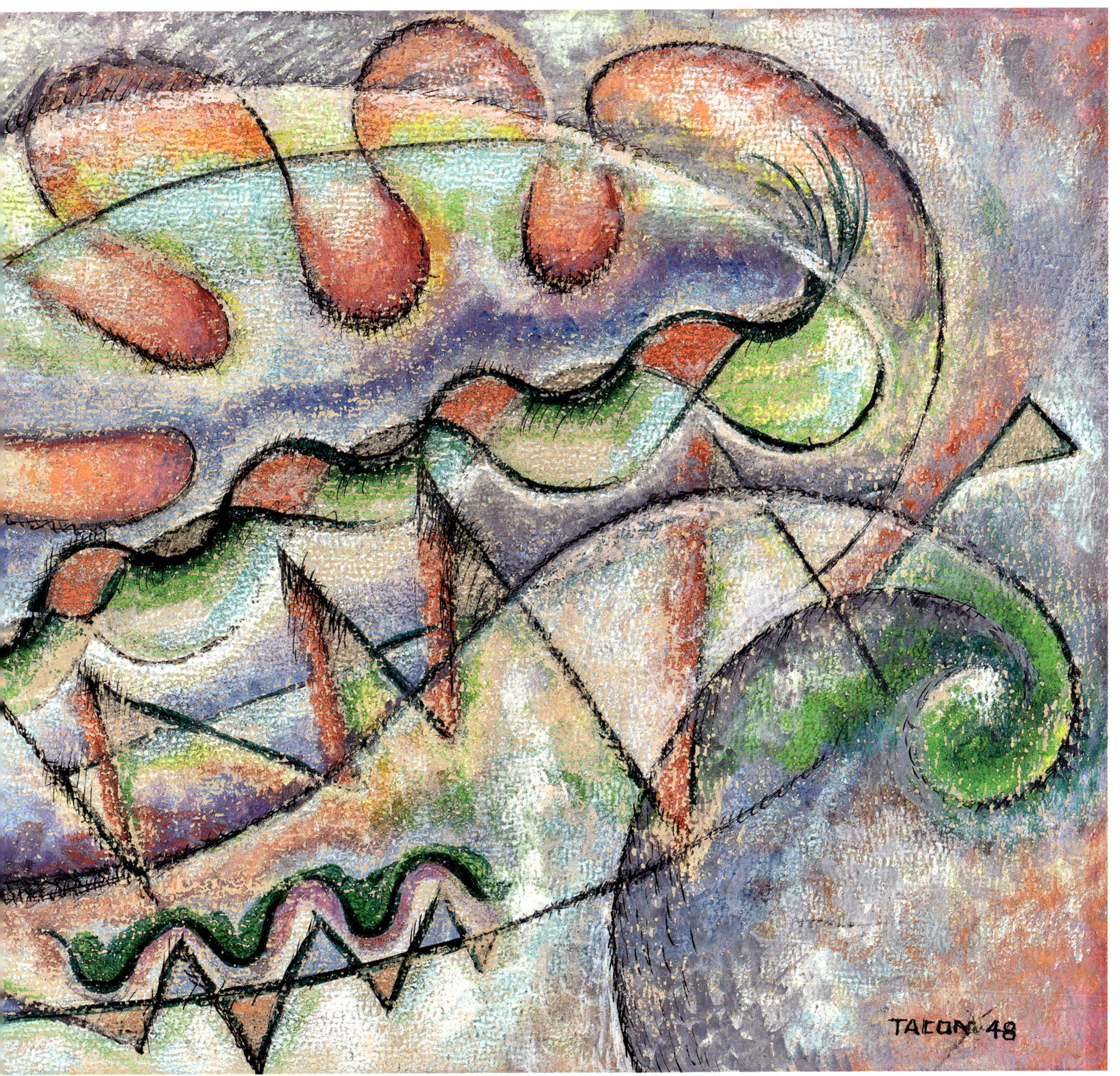
TALON 48

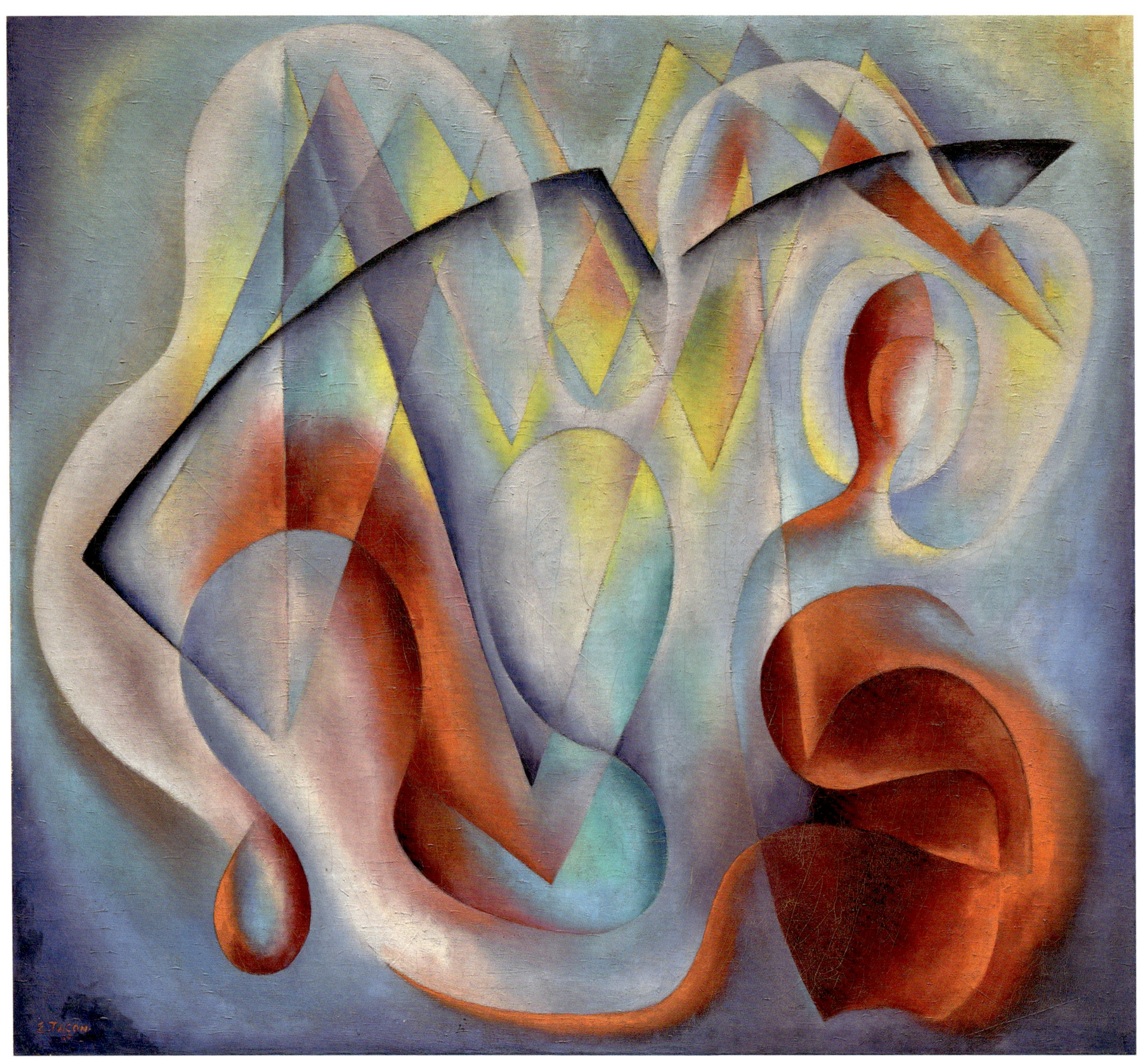

"UNTITLED" 1946–1947

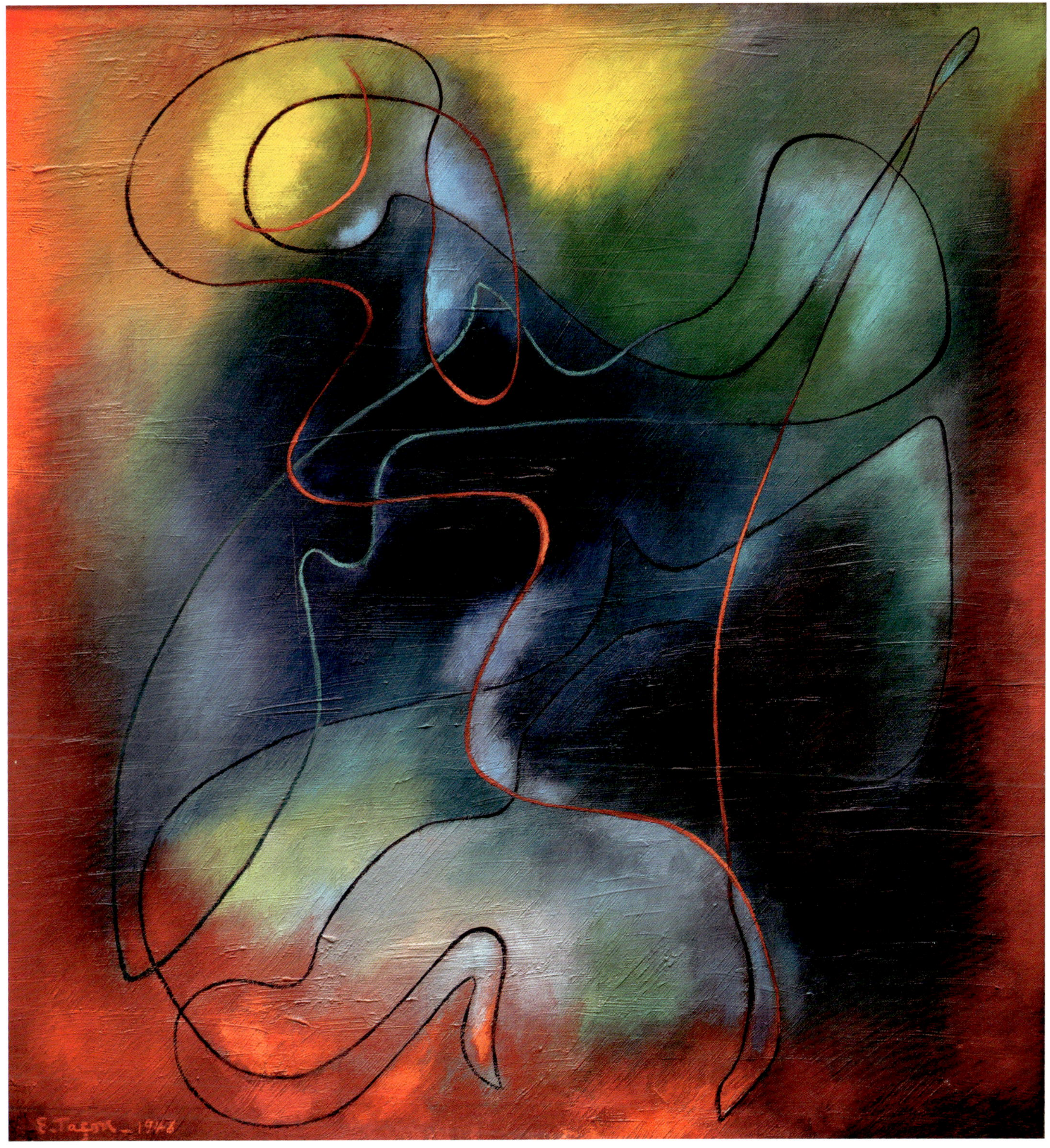

"FLEEING" 1946

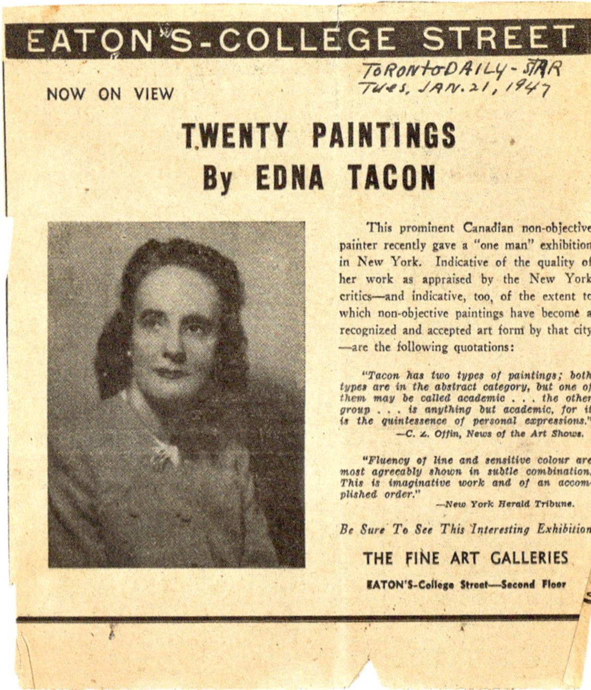

Eaton's ad for *Twenty Paintings by Edna Taçon, January 21, 1947*

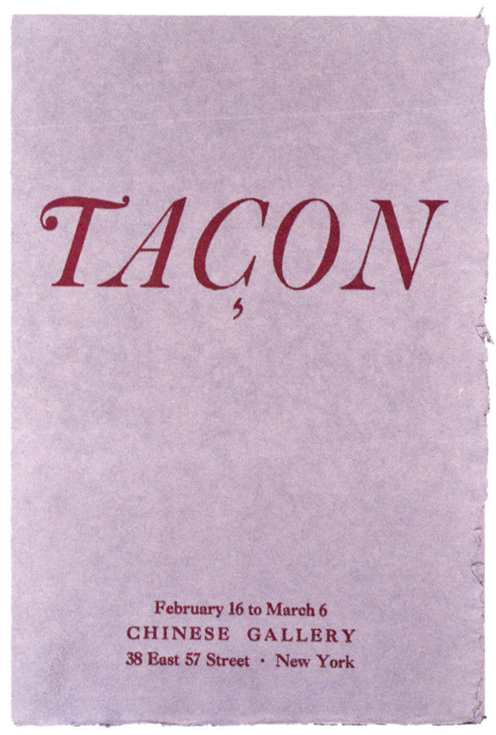

Exhibition pamphlet for *Taçon,*
Chinese Gallery, c. 1946

Exhibition pamphlet for *Edna Taçon: Contextualist,*
Chinese Gallery, 1946

GLOBE + MAIL
JANUARY 25/47

Edna Tacon's Contextualist Art Wins Admiration at Eaton Gallery

By PEARL McCARTHY

The gallery of Edna Tacon's paintings, now on view at Eaton's-College Street, is like a box of sheer aesthetic joy and rare riches. Here, not one or two pieces, but picture after picture consecutively round the walls, reveals new, creative beauty. She produces from the very essence of her artistic vitality. Thus it comes about that, while Edna Tacon's paintings have no recognizable objects from the earthy world, they yet offer the observer a piece of life itself, letting him take ideas and feelings from the artist's vigor, like a kind of transfusion.

Some symbolism may have slipped into Mrs. Tacon's work, but symbolism is not the point. Her pictures, which might be called exquisite metaphors in color and form, relay that moment when the artist's experience of life is transfigured by her own emotional delight in it, so that a verily new and original creation is made. She does not show a picture of a man fleeing after truth in a rich setting of beauty, but she does show, in "Fleeing," how her reaction to that idea added wealth and made a new thing of it. She was right to accept the appellation "contextualist" to describe this amalgam of subjective and objective strands, and it is better to have a label which means something correctly, even though the observer has to dig to find the meaning, than to have a tag of some word which everybody thinks he understands, and doesn't.

There is good work in the exhibition by the Canadian Society of Painters in Water Color, now at the Art Gallery of Toronto. The best piece has everything but a glamorous subject. It is Carl Schaefer's "Carrion Crow," which is not only proficient, but is a prime case of form used to express an idea. (Note those harsh diagonals.) Of contrasting mood, but also an absolute case of "bringing it off," is Rody Kenny Courtice's "Young Hound." The gentle humor of innocence is exuded by the whole form of this dog picture.

David Milne, although in some ways a radical painter, has again the air of an old master in a water color showing, so well integrated in his purpose in the soft-edged glimpse of a city scene, or "The Picture on the Wall," which is an interior by lamplight. B. Cogill Haworth has caught, in "La Calvaire," the complex emotion which is raised when one sees a cemetery with rococo monuments. Representational art is well represented by W. A. Winter's amusing "The Picture Dealer." The vigorous impact of pastel is seen in Leonard Brook's picture of a breakfast table with view through a window beyond. More pieces than can be mentioned have appeal.

88. Paul Duval, "New Qualities Mark Art of Edna Taçon," *Saturday Night* (February 1, 1947).

89. In its March 8 edition, *Saturday Night* published a letter to the editor titled "The Woman Artist" from Peggy Brisby and Anne Sanders, who took exception to Duval's "unfair and incorrect" statement.

90. Duval, "New Qualities Mark Art of Edna Taçon."

91. Letter from the Taçon family archive, October 28, 1947.

pose is a striking example of her professionalism and the respect she demanded as an artist.

The following year, Taçon was praised by critic Paul Duval for her final exhibition at Eaton's. He commented on the gravitas of her work, which he claimed was uncommon in Canada, where most women who exhibited paintings were "non-professional ladies who paint during the holidays as a pastime,"[88] an untrue statement that was later challenged in a letter to the editor.[89] This exhibition included some of the same contextualist paintings as the Chinese Gallery show in New York the previous year. Duval posited that the artist had reached maturity, and described her works as exuding a "gentle, pervading essence" with "a slight kinship to Paul Klee."[90] Another work emblematic of this period is *Untitled* (p.62), in which a figural grouping appears faintly amongst sharp, striated triangles enveloped by a swirling biomorphic form. The palette of this painting is a departure from Taçon's earlier work; here, the blues, reds, and yellows are glowing, high-keyed, and closer to primary hues than in earlier works. In 1948, her last solo exhibition at Chinese Gallery featured work that was much more representational. Taçon became inspired by literary and biblical sources, selecting titles such as *Loaves and Fishes* and *Song of Solomon*. Her approach to content had changed, and after 1948 she took a step back from the art world.

Difficult Choices

In the late 1940s, Taçon's personal life underwent significant change, which may have led to her gradual withdrawal from the art world. In 1947, her marriage ended and she moved permanently to New York. Correspondence from these years reveals that Percy Taçon was determined to keep custody of their sons, Paul and Peter, who were then aged fifteen and eleven, respectively. Edna's letters to Paul from these years are poignant. One letter, which she drafted multiple times before arriving at a final version, assures her sons of her love ("You are constantly in my thoughts"), and explains her necessity to leave: "When you were little boys I felt it would be best for you if I remained with your father, but since circumstances have'nt [sic] improved with the years, I have felt it was wiser to terminate our marriage."[91] Paul never received this letter, instead finding it in his mother's apartment after her death, along with copies of other letters to him. Evidently, all had been intercepted by Percy to portray Edna as having abandoned her sons.

Correspondence from 1949 tells of a legal battle with Percy that kept her from seeing and communicating with her sons. Specifically, a letter from Edna's lawyer, addressed to her second husband, Paul Arnold, indicates that Percy may have threatened her with bigamy charges. Further, it states that Percy would have difficulty in establishing intent, but from the lawyer's "knowledge" of Percy

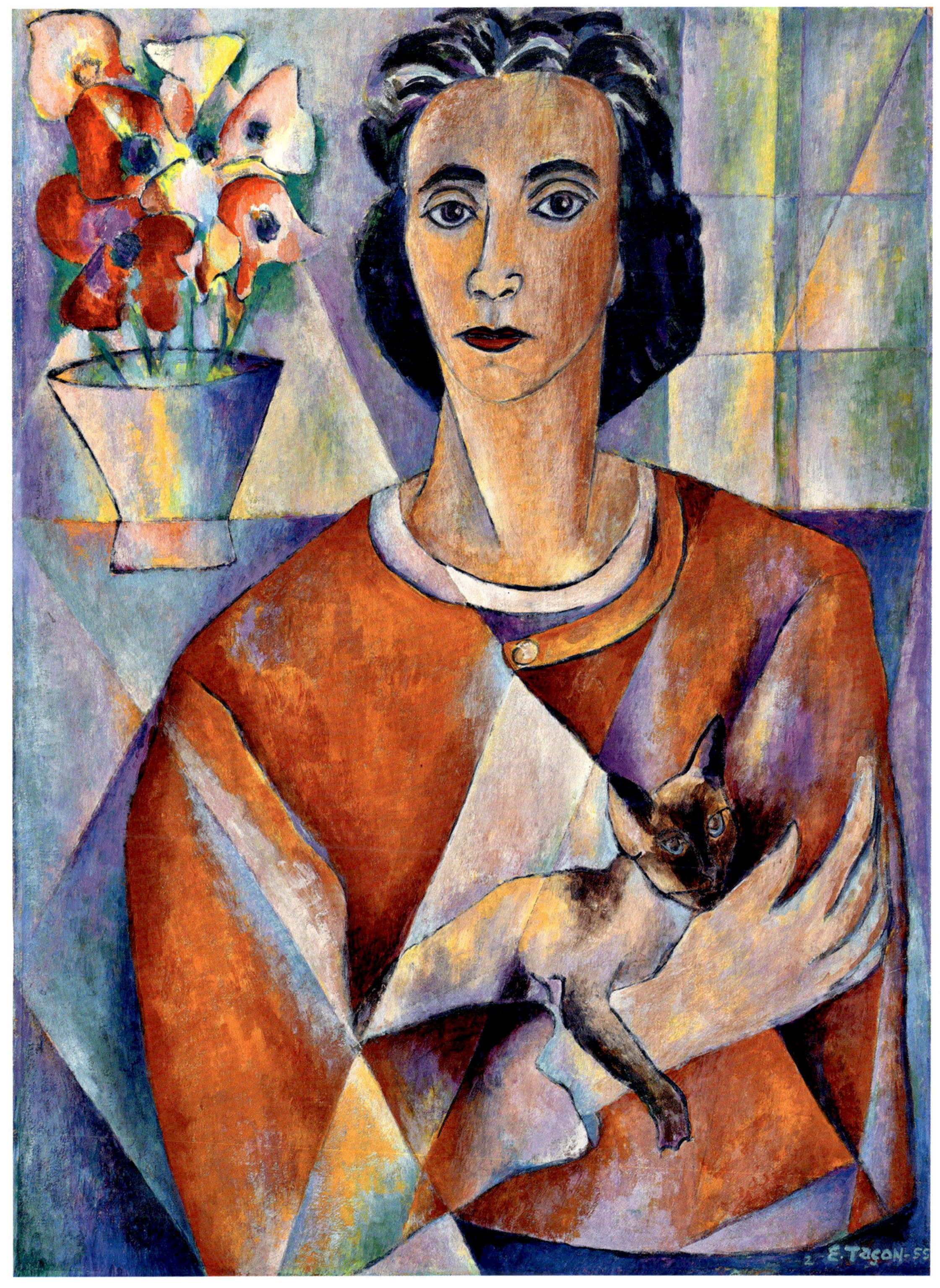

"SELF-PORTRAIT" 1955

92. Letter from the Taçon family archive,
January 1949.

93. Letter from the Taçon family archive,
undated.

94. Diary #1, January 1, 1925.

Taçon, it would not be surprising "if he should in such circumstances lay a charge of bigamy if an opportunity presented itself at some time when Mrs. Taçon is in Canada."[92] The lawyer advised that although the proceedings would not likely result in a conviction, in relation to the children it would be "definitely unwise" for her to return to Canada at that moment. An undated draft letter by Edna addressed to Percy describes her despair and rage from the abuse she endured and that she could not return to Canada to speak in her own defence against his accusations.[93] It is unlikely that this letter was ever sent, perhaps out of her fear of severe consequences for the children, whom she had always sought to protect.

In addition to blocking Edna from returning to Canada, Percy actively disparaged her to others for what he claimed was her decision to "abandon" her children to further her career. Paul had believed this narrative and was estranged from his mother until 1979, when she visited him in Ontario to meet her newborn granddaughter, Claire. The artist, who had legally changed her name to Edna Arnold, spent the final two decades of her life in New York, passing away in 1980 at the age of seventy-five.

Although she and Arnold eventually divorced, she had a close-knit community of friends. The artist surrounded herself with creative types and befriended the famous French mime Marcel Marceau (1923–2007), of whom she painted several portraits. In her later years, Taçon continued to travel through Europe and make paintings, although less frequently and no longer non-objectively. In her late career, she had three retrospective exhibitions in New York: at Charles Z. Mann Gallery (1966, which then travelled to DePauw University in Greencastle, Indiana), Nicholas Roerich Museum (1971) (pp. 70–71), and Harkness House Gallery (1977). Her achievements in Canada were not again recognized until after her death, when art historian Joyce Zemans curated the two-person exhibition *Kathleen Munn and Edna Taçon: New Perspectives on Modernism in Canada* in 1988.

From an art historical perspective, it is important to consider how the domestic abuse and forced separation from her children may have affected Taçon's career and professional ambitions. How did conventional societal structures control the artist's movement through the world and limit her ability to speak out against violence and injustice? Another of her 1925 New Year's resolutions was to "remember I'm always a lady and keep to that position. Not to sully that name by coarse language and improper action."[94] In considering the "decorum" expected of a woman at this time, one must also recognize the amount of courage it took for Taçon to pursue a professional, public-facing career despite the obstacles she faced. How did these barriers impede her success, ultimately erasing her from her rightful and earned place in Canadian art history, even after reaching such heights during her career?

Taçon was a musician first, a professional who, after years of intense study, played concerts and regularly travelled abroad. She translated her musical prowess into non-objective art, where she excelled and led a movement in Canada, forging a path for progressive artists in her wake. All the while, she worked: as a hostess, muralist, educator, milliner, dressmaker, designer, contextualist, mother, and grandmother. She was radical, and she consistently challenged the traditions of art and society. With shards of sinuous forms dancing together, she proposed joy, ethereal beauty, sensuousness, and lightness, without ever compromising her unique vision. ●

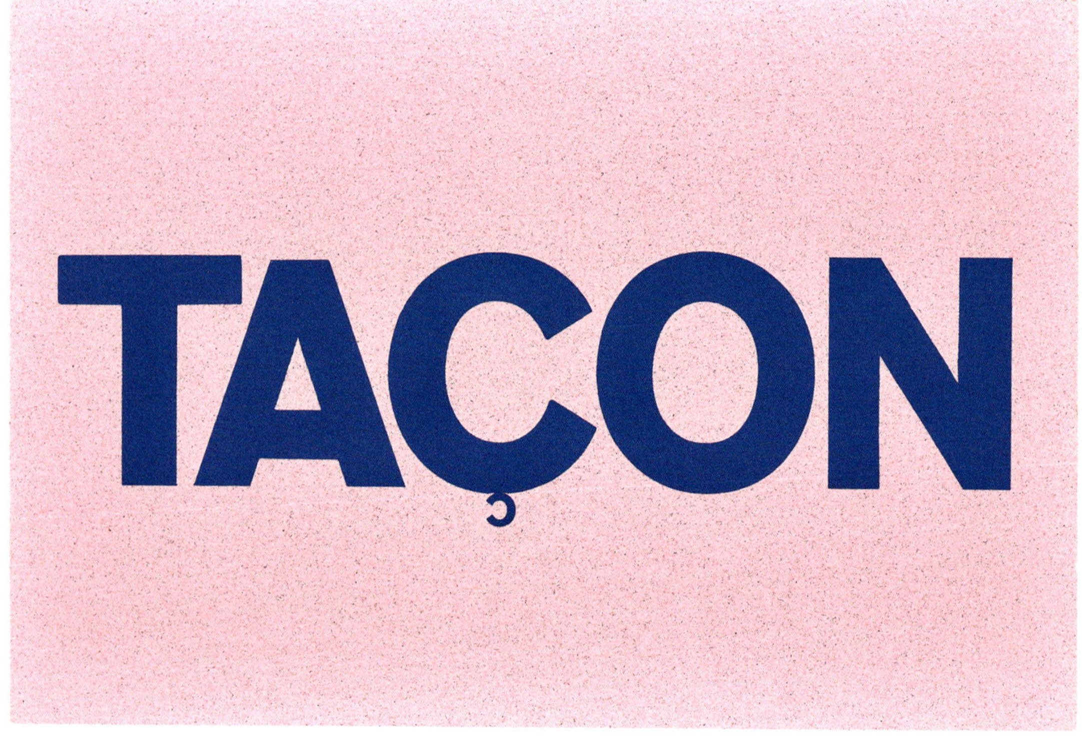

Exhibition pamphlet for *Edna Taçon: Exhibition of Paintings*, Nicholas Roerich Museum, 1971

EDNA TAÇON

EXHIBITION OF PAINTINGS

MARCH 14–APRIL 18

PREVIEW MARCH 14

NICHOLAS ROERICH MUSEUM

DAILY EXCEPT SATURDAY • 2 TO 5 P.M.
NO CHARGE FOR ADMITTANCE

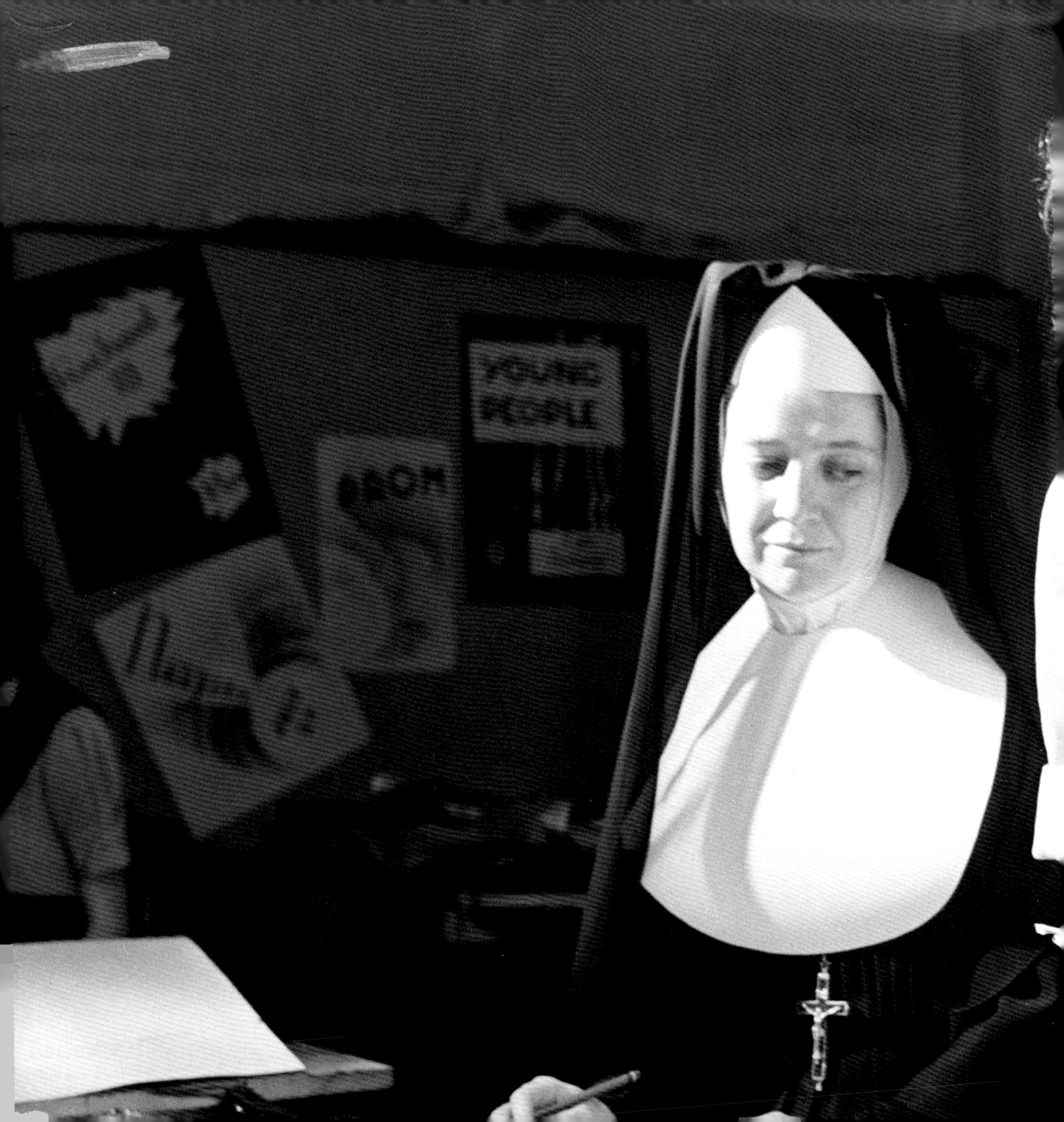
YOUNG
PEOPLE

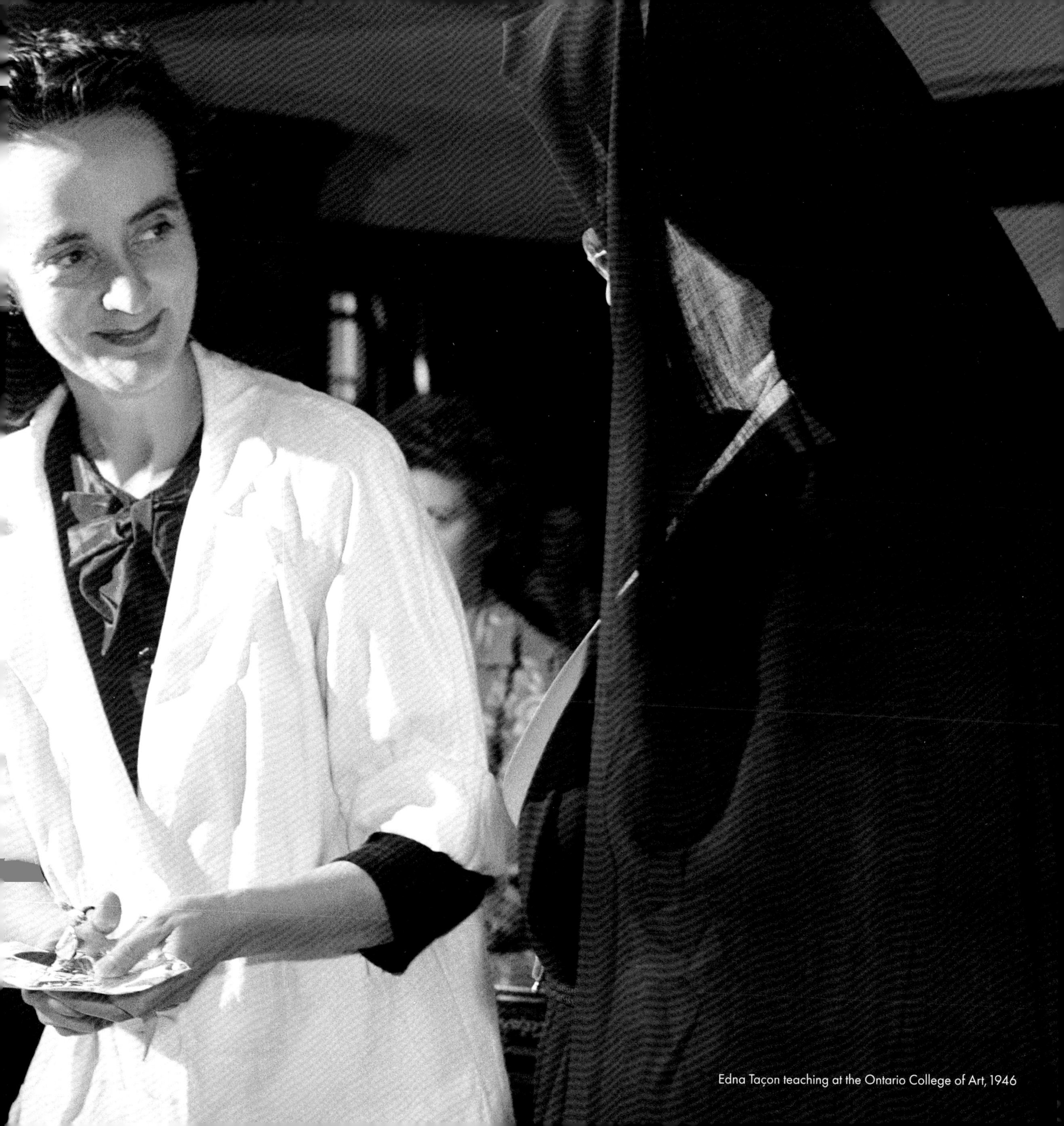

Edna Taçon teaching at the Ontario College of Art, 1946

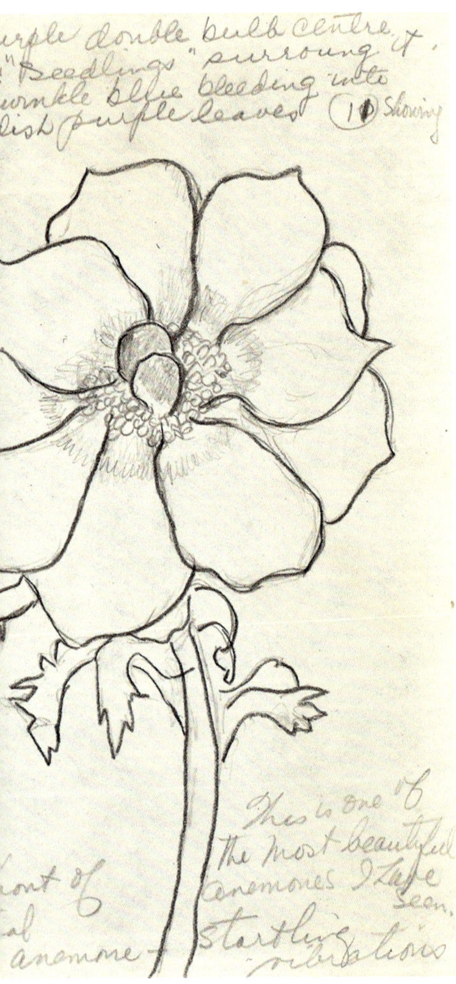

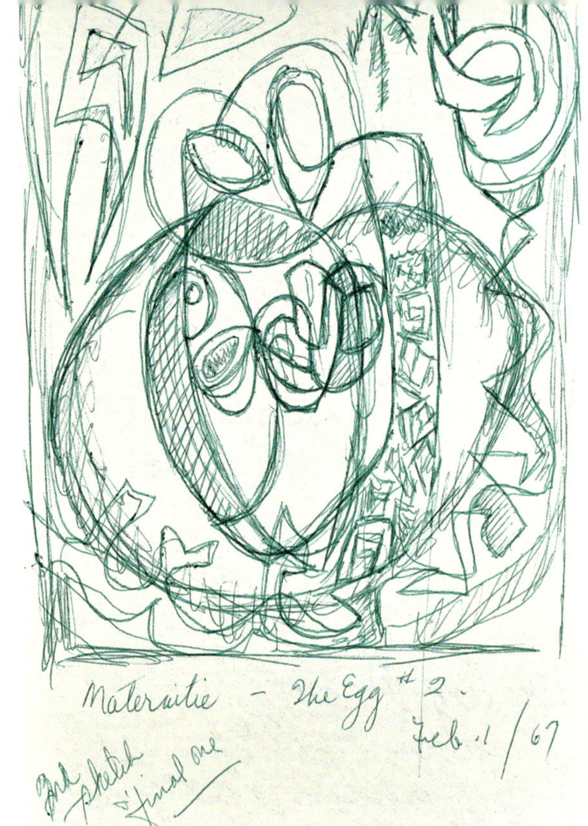

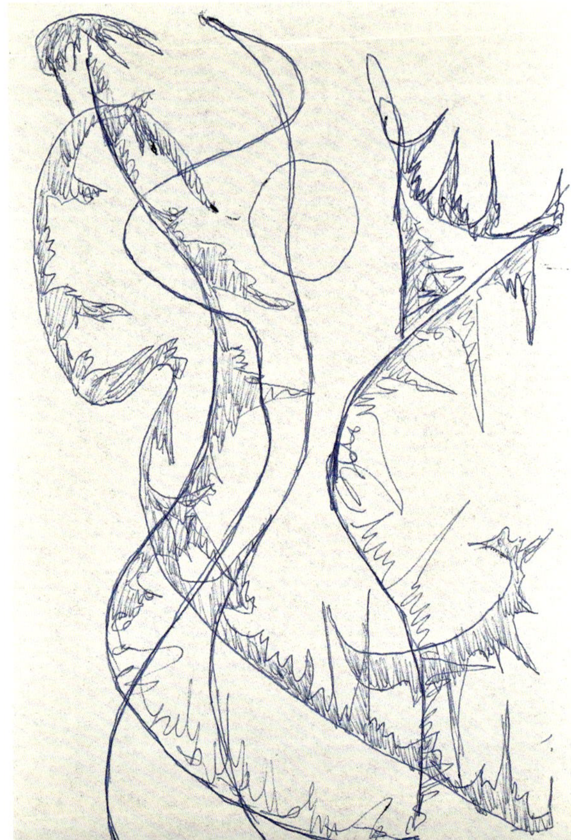

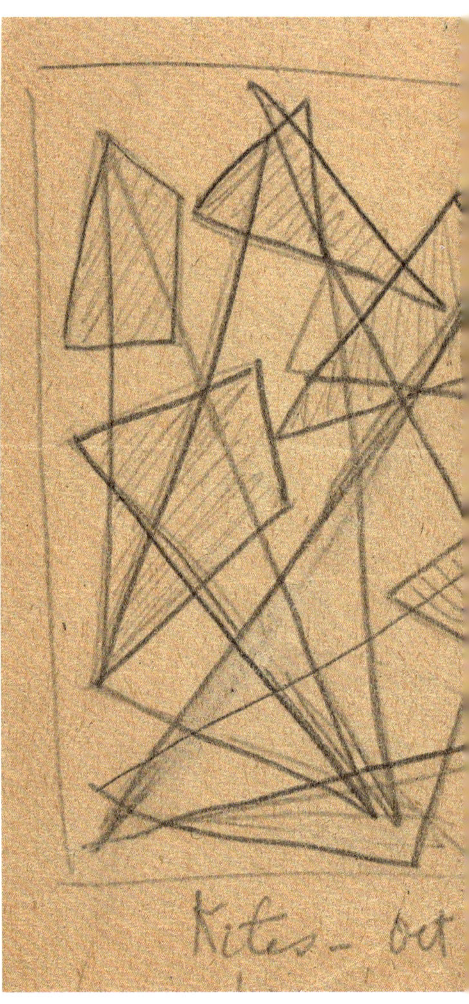

Line flower drawing with notes, c. 1950s
Egg sketch, 1967
Sun and flames sketch, c. 1950s
Kites sketch, 1957

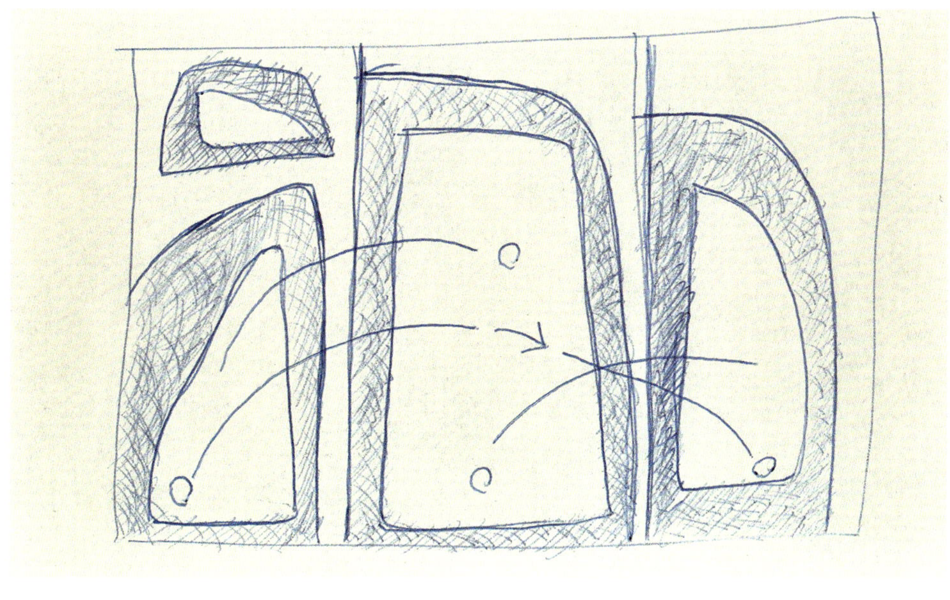

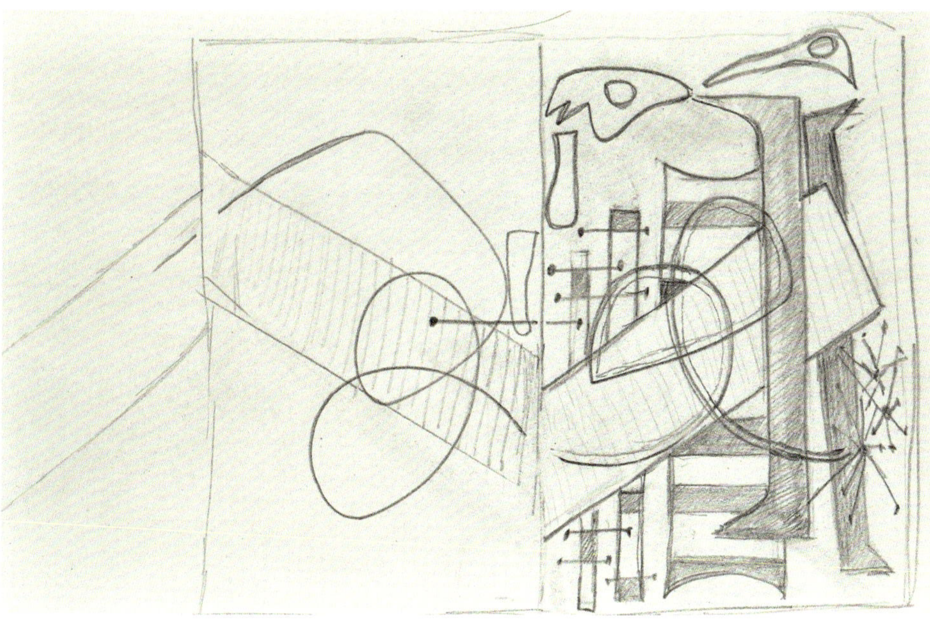

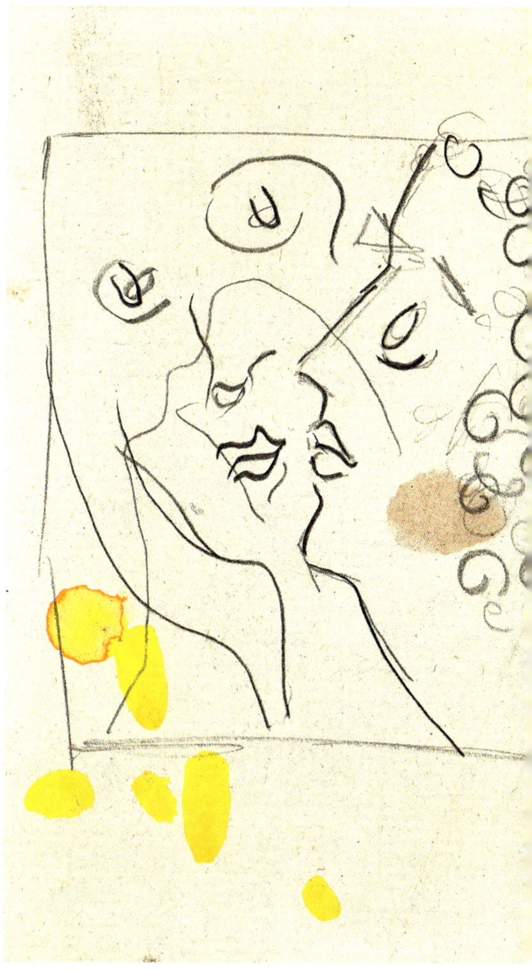

Non-objective sketch 1, c. 1950s
Non-objective sketch 2, c. 1950s
Two faces sketch, c. 1950s

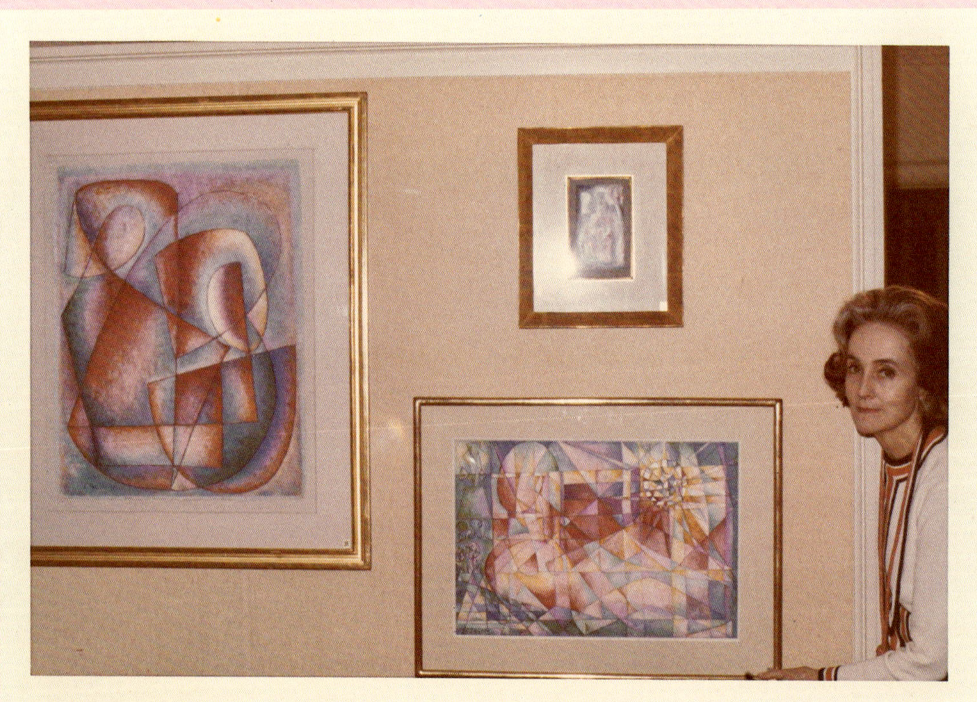

Edna Taçon with her art at home, c. 1971

Carl Taçon &
Renée van der Avoird

Grand-mère: An Interview

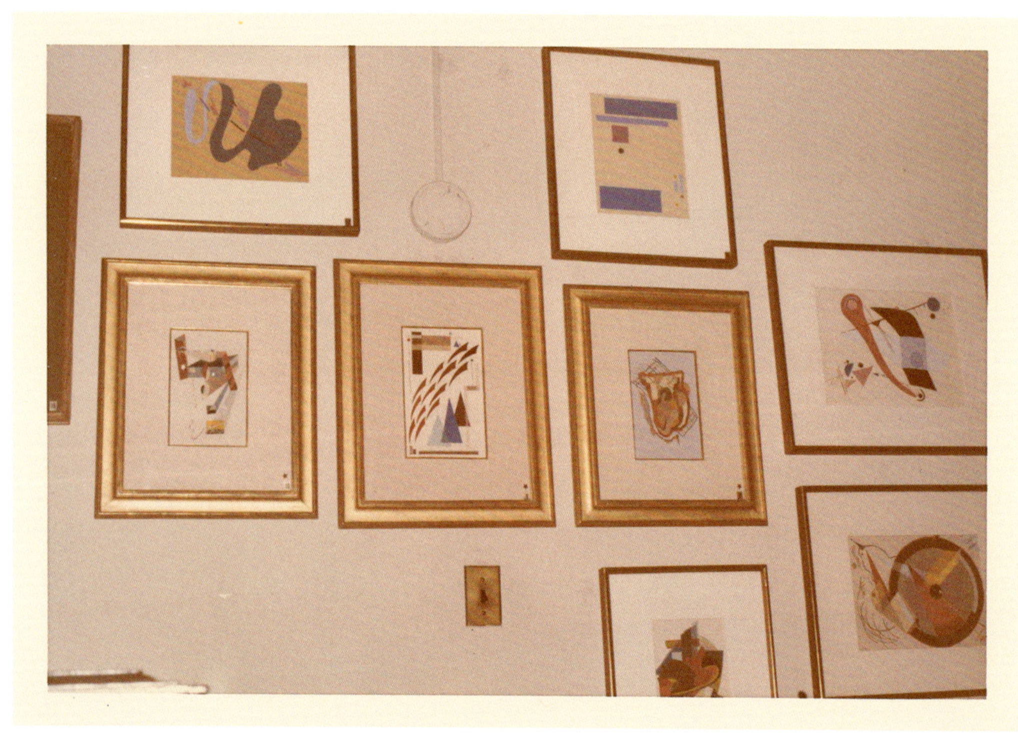

Home interior, c. 1971

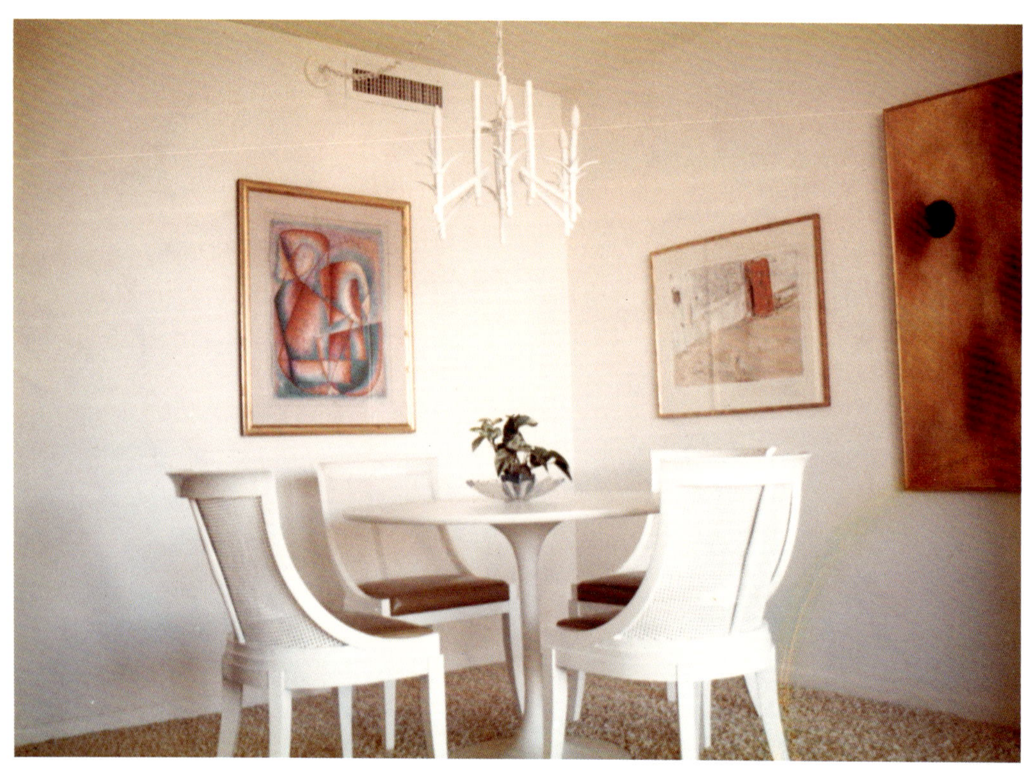

Dining room, c. 1971

Renée van der Avoird: Could you describe some memories of your grandmother?

Carl Taçon: There are a lot of memories from a short period of time, over just a few encounters. When we first met, I was thirteen years old, and I had no idea until just a year prior that I even had a grandmother because of a separation within the family. Remarkably, the first time Edna and I spoke on the phone, it was so comfortable. I felt by the end of the conversation that I had always known her. That wasn't any kind of strange spiritual experience or anything. It was more just a sensation of casual, comfortable interaction.

Edna called me her "moon child" because of my temperament and birth date as a Cancerian. There was something in me she identified with, and she said connected us both. I wondered if that was in part because she had been orphaned and separated from her brother and mother when she was six years old. Edna perhaps associated that with me moving in with my father after my parents separated when I was eight years old, while my older siblings remained living with my mother.

RvdA: When you first visited your grandmother in New York, were you already thinking of being an artist?

CT: I had an interest but no ambition of becoming an artist. When Edna and I went to galleries together in New York, that was a turning point for me, though. It was magical. We went to MoMA to see Picasso's *Guernica*. She talked about her association with the Museum of Non-Objective Painting, and she remembered Jackson Pollock working the door there. Her friends were impressive, such as fashion designer George Halley; Norma Graumann, founder of Brody embroidery; and Marcel Marceau, the famous mime. The things in her apartment amazed me: a Picasso etching, a baby grand piano, her Venetian glass collection, and her own paintings, which hung throughout the apartment, as well as art books and countless cookbooks.

RvdA: I am glad that in her later years, she was able to reconnect with her son and spend time with you, too. After all the struggles, there was that time of happiness for her.

CT: During our first phone call, Edna mentioned that a couple of weeks earlier, she told a friend that she had a dream she reconnected with her family. Shortly thereafter, when my father called her after a thirty-year estrangement, she said her dream had come true. She told me that she always missed her two sons. She always kept a photo of my father as a boy on her dresser from the time she moved to New York.

RvdA: Throughout the 1940s, she made artwork regularly. Her practice slowed in the early 1950s, however, shortly after she permanently moved to New York. Do you know why she took that step away from art-making?

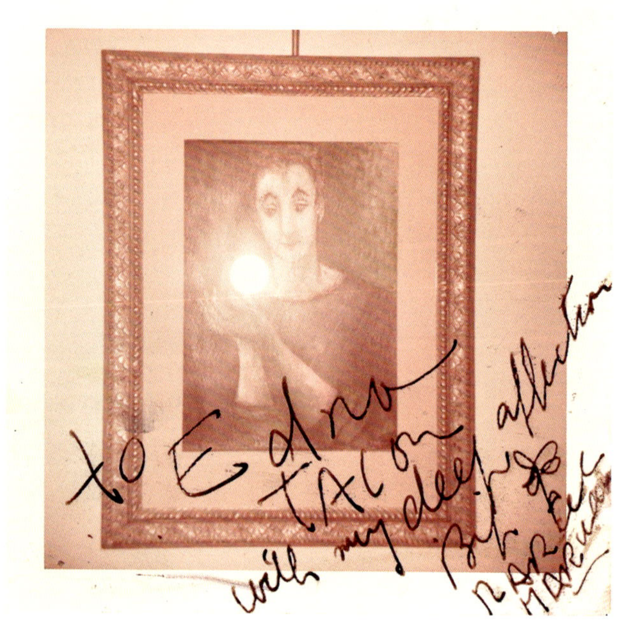

Photograph of portrait of Marcel Marceau by Edna Taçon,
autographed by Marceau, c. 1960

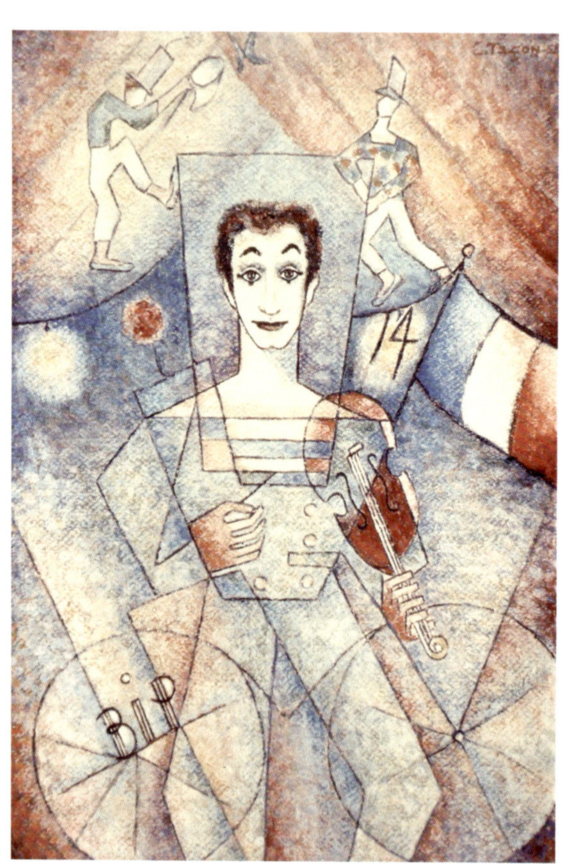

Photograph of painting of Marcel Marceau by
Edna Taçon, 1958

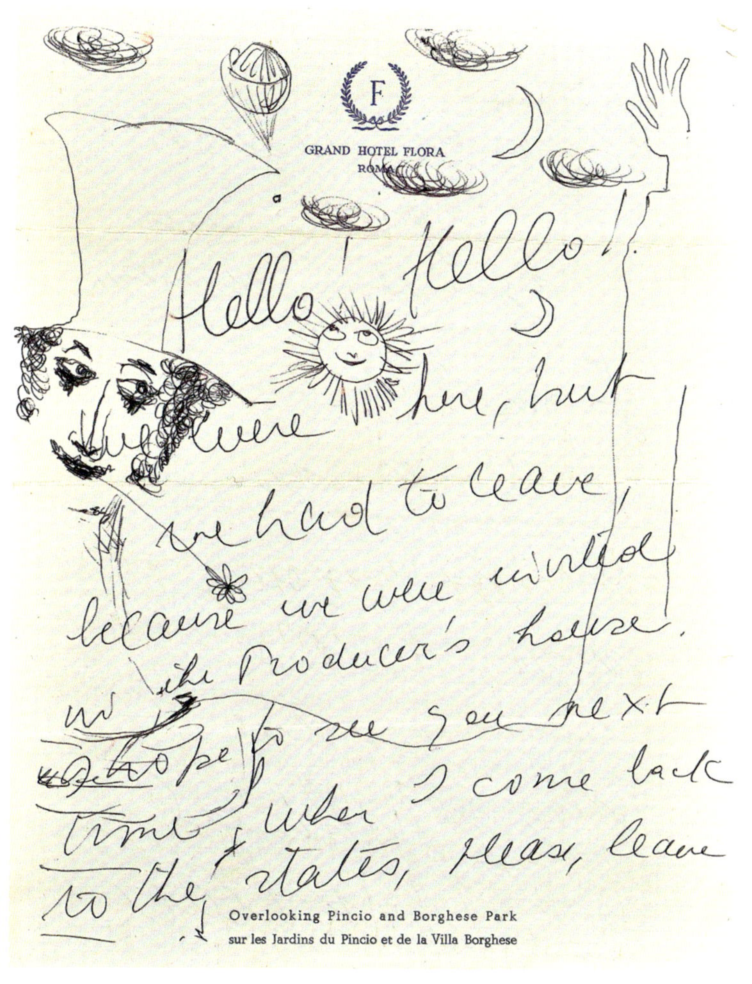

Letter from Marcel Marceau, c. 1960

13 September 1986

Dear Dean Zemans:

Edna Tacon, my grandmother, was the first female, non-objective artist
in Canada. Due to her non-conformist behaviour in a highly conformist
era, she did not receive the recognition in Canada which she deserved.
For example, she was a feminist starting a career in the 1930's when
feminism was regarded virtually as pathological. She divorced in the
mid-1940's when divorce was frowned upon and, a Christian, she
remarried a Jew. Finally, in 1948, she moved to New York where,
notwithstanding her artistic success there, her Canadian identity was
obscured.

My objective is to organize a travelling national exhibition of her
paintings, accompanied by a book catalogue. It is my belief that her
contribution and significance to Canadian art history and the feminist
movement is extremely substantial and, as this has not been properly
recorded, it leaves a sizable gap in Canadian art history.

Attached are some photocopies of articles written about my grandmother
and her work and a simplified curriculum vitae which I have taken from
her art scrapbook.

I ask for your assistance in the initiation of such a project. Your
suggestions and support would be welcome.

I would also add that Professor Hugh LeRoy indicated that he strongly
supports this project and wishes to cosign this request.

I look forward to hearing from you.

Yours truly,

Carl Tacon

Letter from Carl Taçon to
Joyce Zemans, 1986

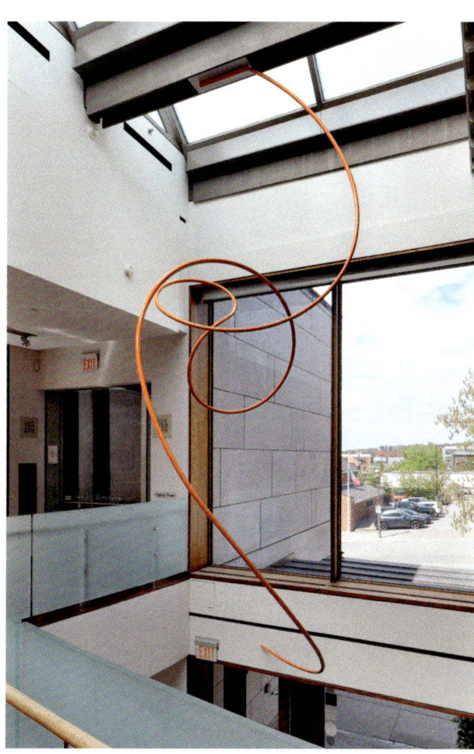

CT: The late 1940s and early '50s were a transitional time during which her work changed. She found herself in a position where she was suddenly supported both emotionally and financially by her second husband, Paul Arnold, after her traumatic breakup with Percy Taçon. With Percy, it was a professional relationship, too; they shared an artistic circle, and when things were going well between the two of them, they spurred each other on. When she moved to New York, she lost that camaraderie as well. It was a time when women didn't have rights, particularly if they left their marriage. She lost the rights to her kids. Apparently, she had a trunk full of mementos, sketches, and personal things that she had left with Percy in Toronto, and he destroyed those. He tarnished her reputation, so there wasn't a lot for her to come back to in Toronto.

RvdA: In 1986, you introduced art historian Joyce Zemans to your grandmother's work and asked for her assistance in organizing a nationally touring exhibition. That project came to fruition in 1988 with the exhibition *Kathleen Munn and Edna Taçon: New Perspectives on Modernism in Canada* at the Art Gallery of York University, which travelled to six other venues across Canada. Can you explain what motivated you to write that letter to Dr. Zemans (left) while you were an undergraduate student?

CT: Edna seemed to have been lost in time, and I felt there was a contribution that she had made to the Canadian art scene, but there wasn't a lot of information about her.

One of the professors that I had at York was painter Ronald Bloore. He knew Edna and Percy when he was quite young and was very interested in their work at the time. He said they suddenly vanished. He didn't know what had happened. When I had enrolled in a class with him, he had recognized the name. He said, "Are you related to Percy and Edna Taçon?" I said, "Yes, I'm their grandchild." Ron questioned why her work was no longer celebrated. Another professor of mine, sculptor Hugh LeRoy, felt that something should be done to try and have an exhibition of her work and more research done on her. I knew that Joyce Zemans was interested in, and was researching, female Canadian artists, so I wrote her that letter. She then stopped me one day when I was walking past the Dean's office and asked, "Why didn't you tell me about your grandmother?" It confirmed that people recognized Edna, and they wondered why she was no longer known.

RvdA: Edna was American by birth. Do you think she felt she belonged more in the United States than in Canada?

CT: She saw herself as both Canadian and American. By the time I met her, she had been in New York permanently for over thirty years and she was

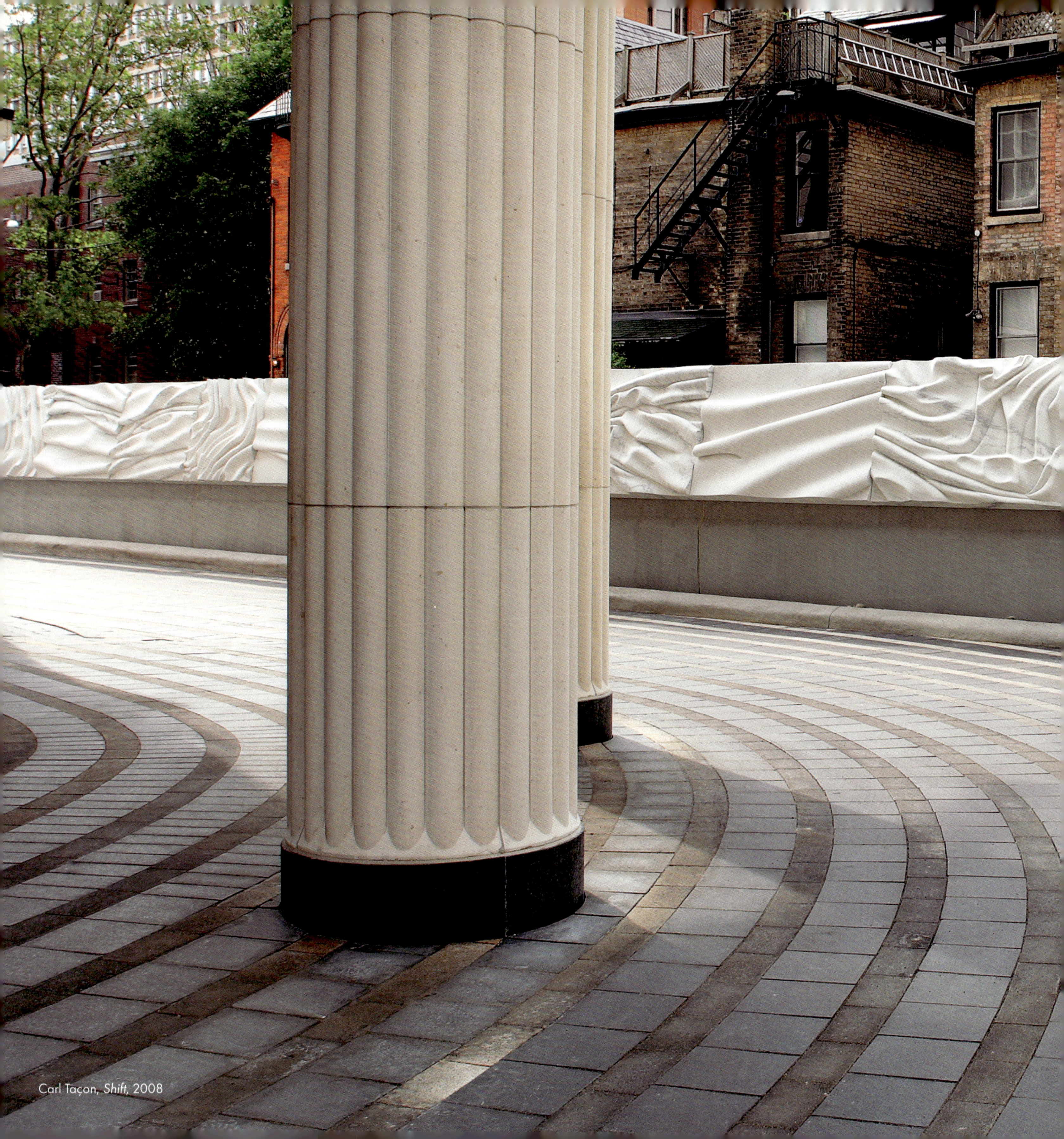

Carl Taçon, *Shift*, 2008

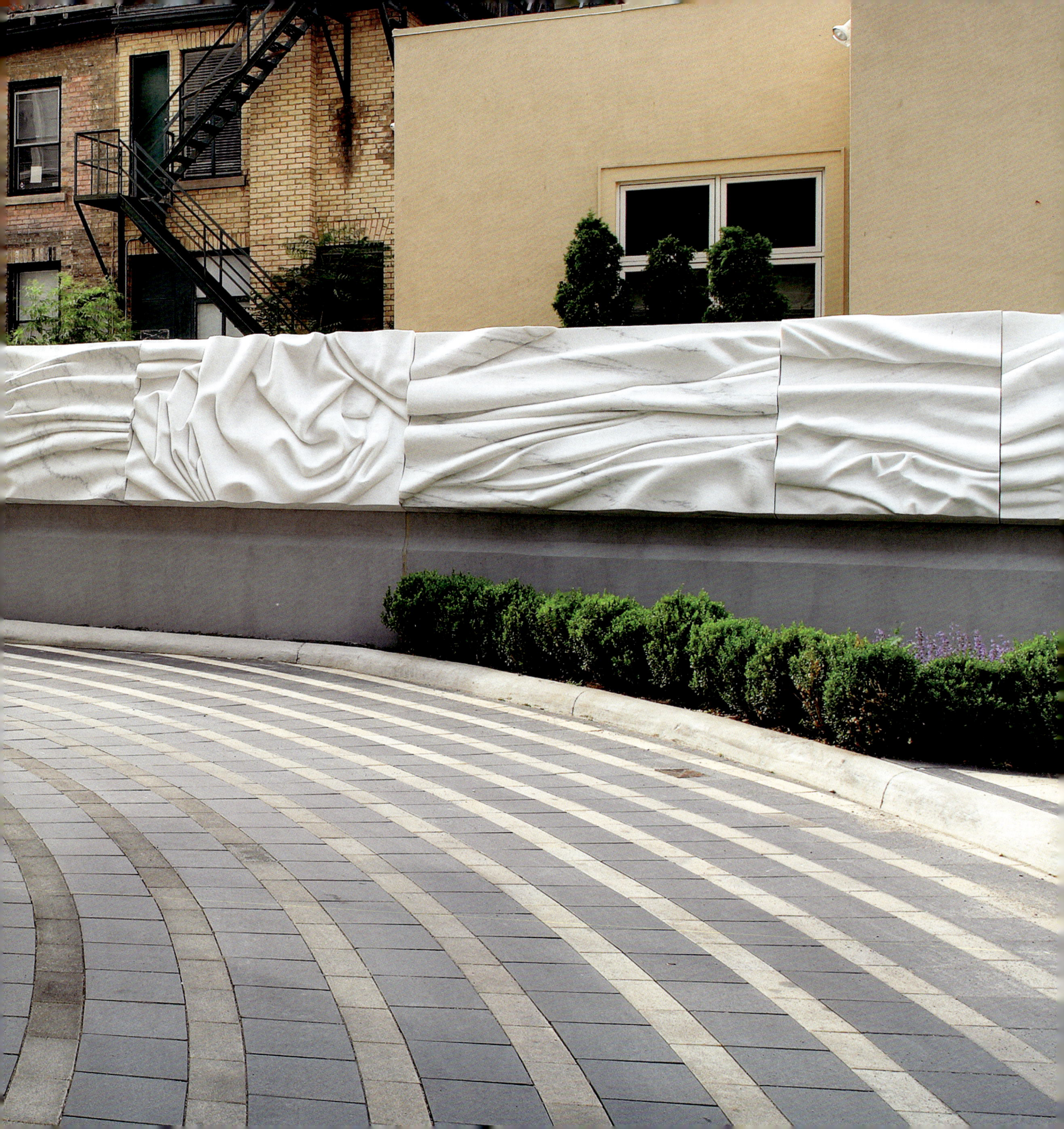

THE EVENING TELEGRAM

DAILY CIRCULATION, JUNE 183,988

TORONTO, THURSDAY, JULY 25, 1946

SECOND SECTION

Taxpayer 'Has No Chance' To Win An Income Appeal Fleming Asks Real Board

Toronto Members Urge Action Now to Curb Powers of Revenue Minister

By L. M. McKECHNIE
Telegram Staff Reporter

Ottawa, July 25—The broad discretionary power conferred on the Minister of National Revenue under the Income Tax and Excess Profits Tax Acts has an appealing taxpayer "licked before he starts," Donald Fleming, Progressive Conservative member for Eglinton, complained in the House of Commons yesterday as he urged some real method of appeal against the minister's arbitrary rulings.

Mr. Fleming, supported by Harry Jackman (PC, Rosedale) and several other members, launched a determined attack on the procedure which puts the taxpayer in the position of appealing "from Caesar unto Caesar." The situation was so acute, he said, that it would not wait another year and demanded immediate remedial action.

But the agitation only won an assurance from Acting Finance Minister Douglas Abbott that a "committee" now studying revision of the Income Tax Act would make every effort to reduce the discretionary powers of the minister. To allow any appeal from a ruling by the minister as the result of the exercise of his discretionary power, Mr. Abbott argued, would be "a negation of the principle of ministerial responsibility."

The discussion came toward the end of a day devoted entirely to consideration of the government budget resolutions in committee of ways and means. During the two sittings of the day the House in committee progressed only as far as to give approval to eight of 37 resolutions involving amendments to the Income Tax Act.

FAR AND WIDE

The debate ranged far and wide and the chairman frequently had to jerk members back from meandering into such remote fields as the cost of nursing service, the taxation methods of the Trojans and a tax on juke boxes.

Mr. Fleming made the major constructive criticisms when he started the day by describing the compulsory acceptance of family allowances as "interference with individual liberties," and ended the sitting with his attack on the discretionary powers allowed the Minister of National Revenue.

His principal complaint was voiced when the committee considered proposals to establish two new boards under the Income Tax Act, one (the income tax appeal board), to which taxpayers may appeal ministerial de-

Gangs All Quit Won't Dig Hole Builder Needs

Regina, July 25 — (CP) — One Regina home-owner is wondering whether his attempt to ease the housing shortage is worth the effort. His plan to convert his three-storey house into two suites necessitated building a small ground floor addition which in turn required a small excavation.

This is what happened when he sought labor.

1. The men engaged three weeks ago to do the job failed to show up.
2. Another gang was employed and they quit.
3. Operators of mechanized excavating equipment found the space too confined for their equipment.
4. The next groups of laborers hired quit to take on a larger project.

There is still no hole in the ground.

DOMINION DAY NAME CHANGE GETS SUPPORT

Government Leader in Senate, Backing Quebec Plea, Wants July 1 Called National Holiday of Canada

Ottawa, July 25—(CP)—Hon. Wishart Robertson, government leader in the Senate and member of the Cabinet, supported second reading of the Canada Day bill in the Upper House in the hope that when it was further studied in committee it would be amended to call the July 1 holiday—the national holiday of Canada.

This was modified support for a suggestion from Senator Lorimer Gouin (L.-Quebec) that the day be called—the National Day. And it was the first time the government leader had come out in support of the idea of changing the name of the holiday from Dominion Day.

Senator Robertson had stated in his speech that he did not think the changing of the name from Dominion Day to Canada Day would serve the purpose for which it was desired—to ensure proper observance of the day.

Some Husbands Pick Wives' Hats, Others Just Pay And Ignore 'Em

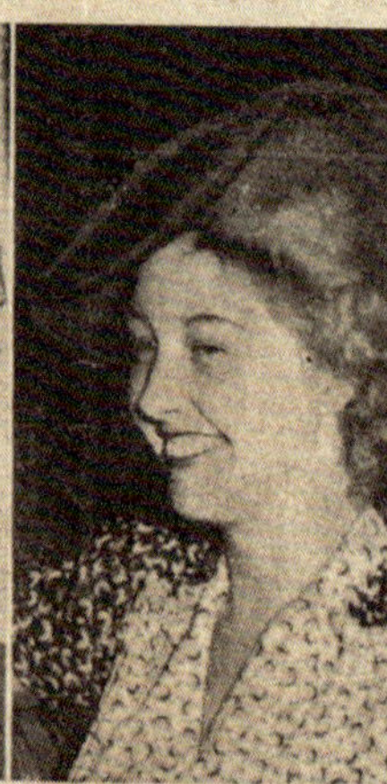

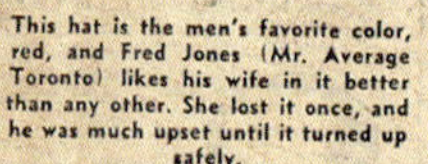

Mrs. Robert Saunders, wife of Toronto's Mayor, wears a turquoise blue hat her husband likes. Much like the Queen's favorite style, it increases Mrs. Saunders' resemblance to Her Majesty.

This hat is the men's favorite color, red, and Fred Jones (Mr. Average Toronto) likes his wife in it better than any other. She lost it once, and he was much upset until it turned up safely.

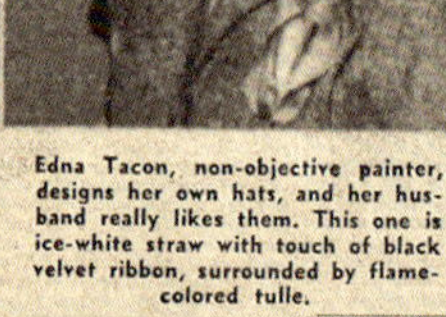

Edna Tacon, non-objective painter, designs her own hats, and her husband really likes them. This one is ice-white straw with touch of black velvet ribbon, surrounded by flame-colored tulle.

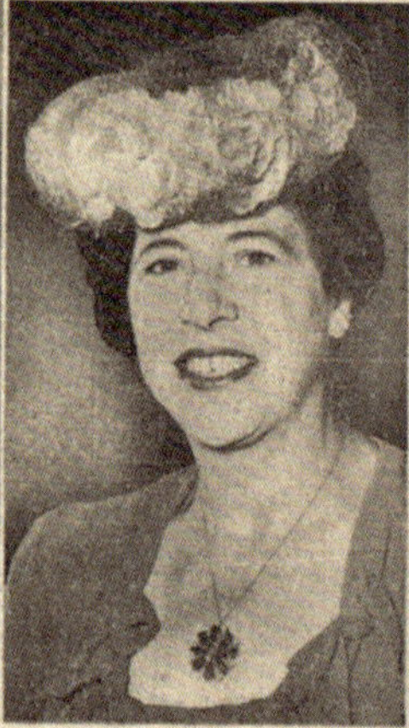

Mrs. Fred Hawes, wife of "Frederic", one of Canada's better known hat designers, is sure her husband likes her hats, for he creates them. She wears a 'circle of shell-pink roses covered with bronze veil.

By DOROTHY HOWARTH
Telegram Staff Reporter

HANG on to your hats, ladies! H. M. Cowan, executive director of Fashion Industries, says the reason women's hats are as they are is because women spend most of their time figuring out new ways to outdo each other.

"If one has a hat with a 10-inch brim, her friend has to have one with a 12-inch," and Mr. Cowan will not criticize this innocent rivalry. Broken down, added up and rebaked it is what he eats for dinner.

Such expert opinion cannot be accepted without careful investigation—investigation of the critic who not only has to endure the hat, but pay the price. What do men think of women's hats, particularly their wives? . . .

The investigation went something like this:

"Good morning Mr. Smith. This

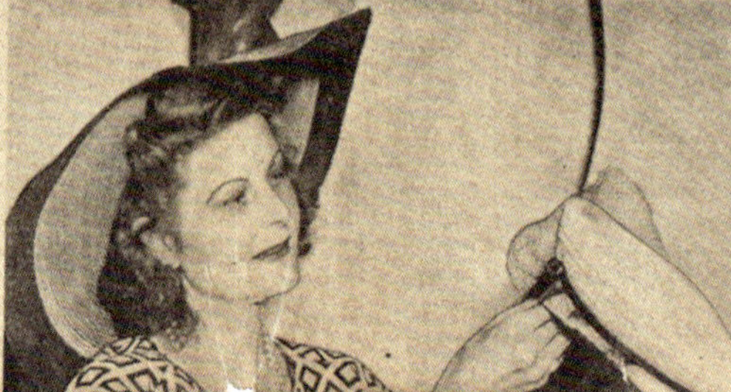

UNRRA Nearing Wind-Up Through When Funds Gone

Spy Probe Talk Tires Caretaker Turns Out Lights

Ottawa, July 25 — (CP) — A tired caretaker brought a rapid conclusion to a meeting of the Ottawa Civil Liberties Association, called to discuss the Royal Commission report on espionage.

The meeting, held in Dominion United Church, ignored the turning out of a caution light and launched

United Nations Might Fill Gap For Countries Still Needing Aid—Distress Diminishes

Washington, July 25—(CP)—Operations of the United Nations Relief and Rehabilitation Administration will definitely end with exhaustion of appropriations for the current year and the winding up process will be a major subject of discussion at the council meeting scheduled to open in Geneva, August 5.

A second major problem at the

---

happy there. At that time, she was established as a New Yorker. Although, she had the demeanour of a more humble, modest Canadian, not the grit of a New Yorker. I think she had a strong connection to both places.

However, in terms of her identity, I think secretly she wished she was French. Even when I first visited her, she told me that she didn't want to be called anything like "Grandmother" or "Grandma." She said, "Definitely not Granny or Nana." She would only accept being called *Grand-mère*.

RvdA: In her diary, she calls her music lessons *leçons* with the cedilla.

CT: She also had lots of French cookbooks. She taught me how to make a French recipe called "Shrimps-in-Love."

RvdA: How do you think the complexity of her identity affected the artwork that she made, if at all?

CT: Her disciplined manner of studying and performing music gave a certain structure to the way she worked. I think that applied to her life in general. She was motivated and task-oriented, traits that came out in her artwork, which is very detailed. Perhaps the intensity of working—of making art—was an escape from early traumas and changes in her life: losing her father, being adopted, moving to Goderich and then to Toronto. I think often one's work becomes a kind of escape, a way of processing and focusing.

One thing she indirectly taught me, through visiting her and seeing her apartment, was to rejoice in beauty and to find pleasure in small things. Not just momentous things. While travelling in Italy or France, she would buy little objects in stores. Paul Arnold would say, "Why do you buy all these little things? Why don't you just buy something big for yourself?" She said she was always interested in lots of little things.

RvdA: That's interesting to hear because the collages, to me, are assemblages of tiny shards coming together in accumulations of aesthetically pleasing forms. Some of her paintings are like that in a way, too— beautiful things gathered together.

CT: She was very attracted to the decorative, whether that was through her artwork, embroidery, or fashion. She had some amazing dresses. Really flamboyant ones. And of course, there were her handmade hats (left).

RvdA: In her diaries from the 1920s, she comes across as energetic and strong-willed. I wonder if you think these personality traits contributed to her success as an artist.

CT: Edna was extremely passionate about her work as both a musician and painter. Her passion allowed her to persevere in a male-dominated environment which, more often than not, trivialized female artists. While she was soft-spoken, she was very determined. Any artist wants to move ahead in their career, and she would want that recognition, but I think her true passion was in the process of making art and music. That was perhaps her greatest strength.

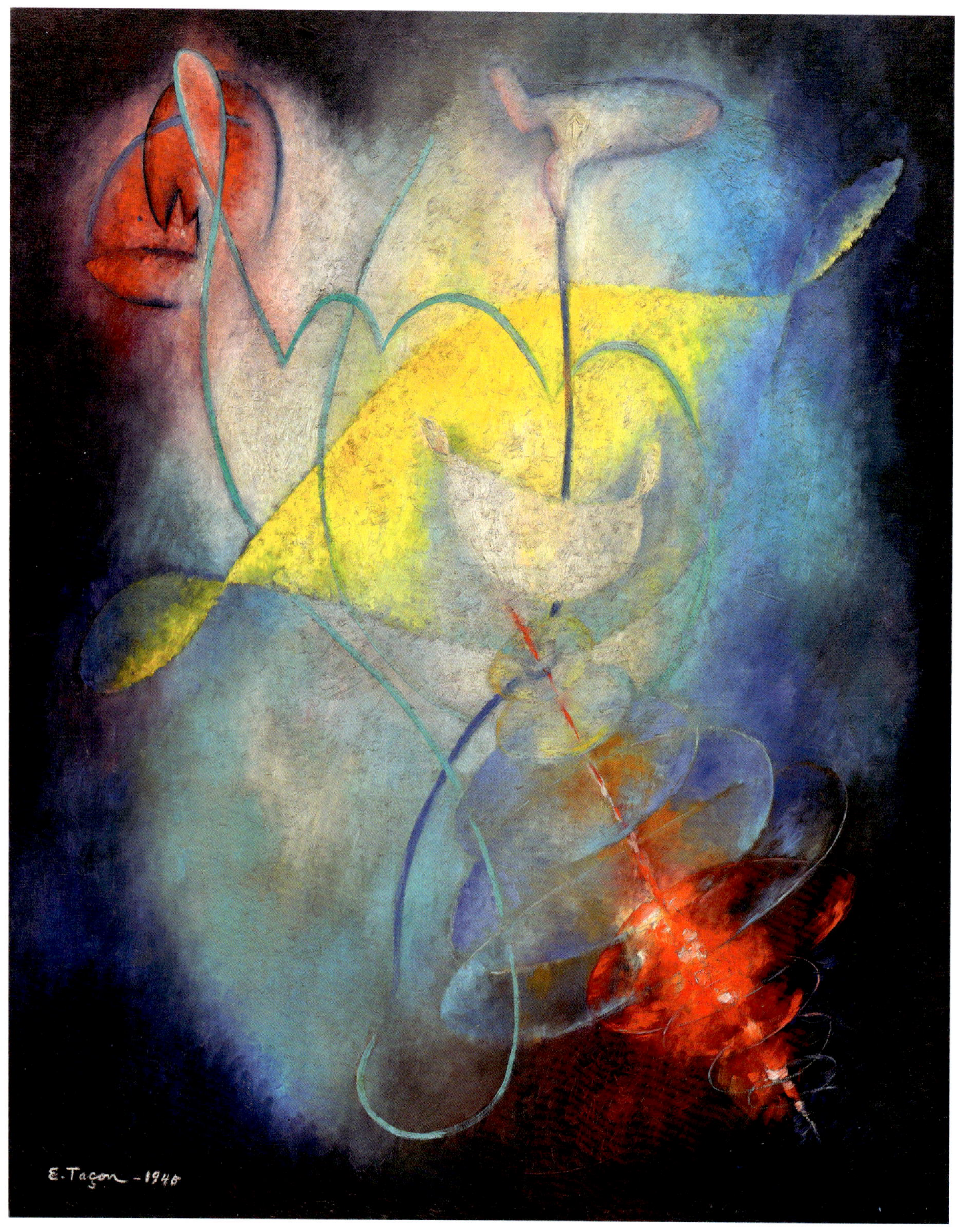

"AURORA" 1945

RvdA: Has your own artwork been influenced by Edna's?

CT: There is undoubtedly a relationship, and it comes out in subtle ways through a shared interest in line and edge, and how those elements play into composition. For me, line and edge are translated both in my flat and three-dimensional works, like the sculptures *Grace Note* and *Shift* (p. 83 and pp. 84–85).

RvdA: Both *Grace Note* and *Shift* are quite different from Edna's work in terms of scale and material, but there is a visual connection.

CT: *Grace Note* is more linear, but *Shift* is a pictorial piece with separate compositions working together. At times, Edna incorporated what appeared to be drapery folds into her work. There is also a rhythmic nature to her work, like music changing as it moves along a line. Part of the way *Shift* has been constructed is that the edge line of the profile, where the drapery folds over, reaches the edge of the panel. That line is meant to be visible and not match the next panel so that viewers are aware of those edges.

RvdA: There is something so precious about our relationships with grand-mothers. It's almost as though grandmothers can be freer with their grandchildren than they had been with their own children. I sense that your bond with Edna was profound but also fun.

CT: She was playful, and I have many stories that remind me of her mischievous side. Once, she served a type of sweet corn that I had never tried before — a hybrid variety that she had bought at a local vegetable store in New York. I liked it so much that she packed six cobs in my suitcase so that I could smuggle them across the border into Canada and try growing my own.

RvdA: Oh, your *Grand-mère*! Did you try to grow it?

CT: I tried but nothing happened. It didn't grow. It probably was a variety that couldn't be grown here.

RvdA: It was a hybrid, just like her. I love that spirit—her sending you home, covertly, with something to grow.

CT: I would have liked to experience more of that spirit. ●

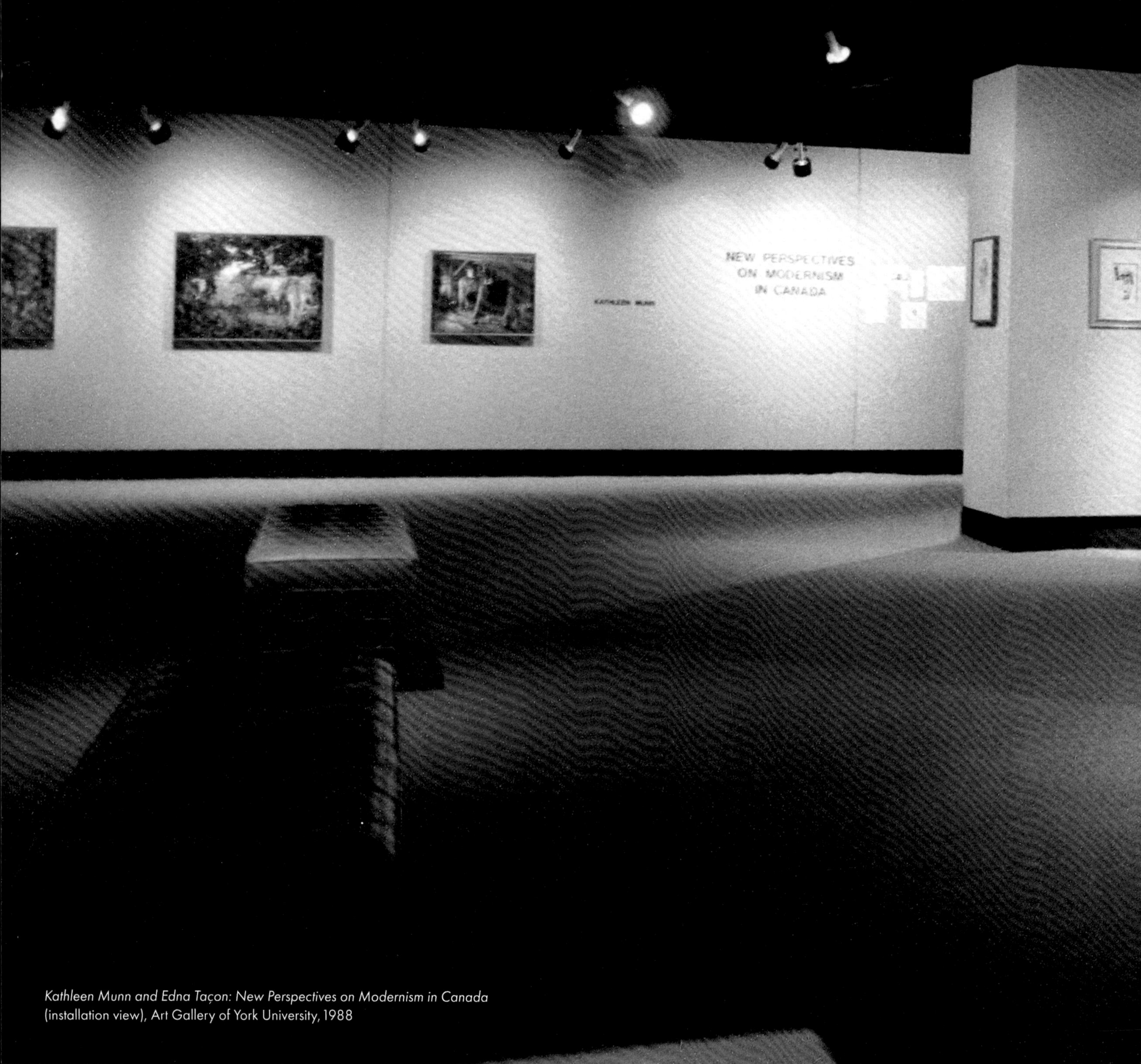

Kathleen Munn and Edna Taçon: New Perspectives on Modernism in Canada (installation view), Art Gallery of York University, 1988

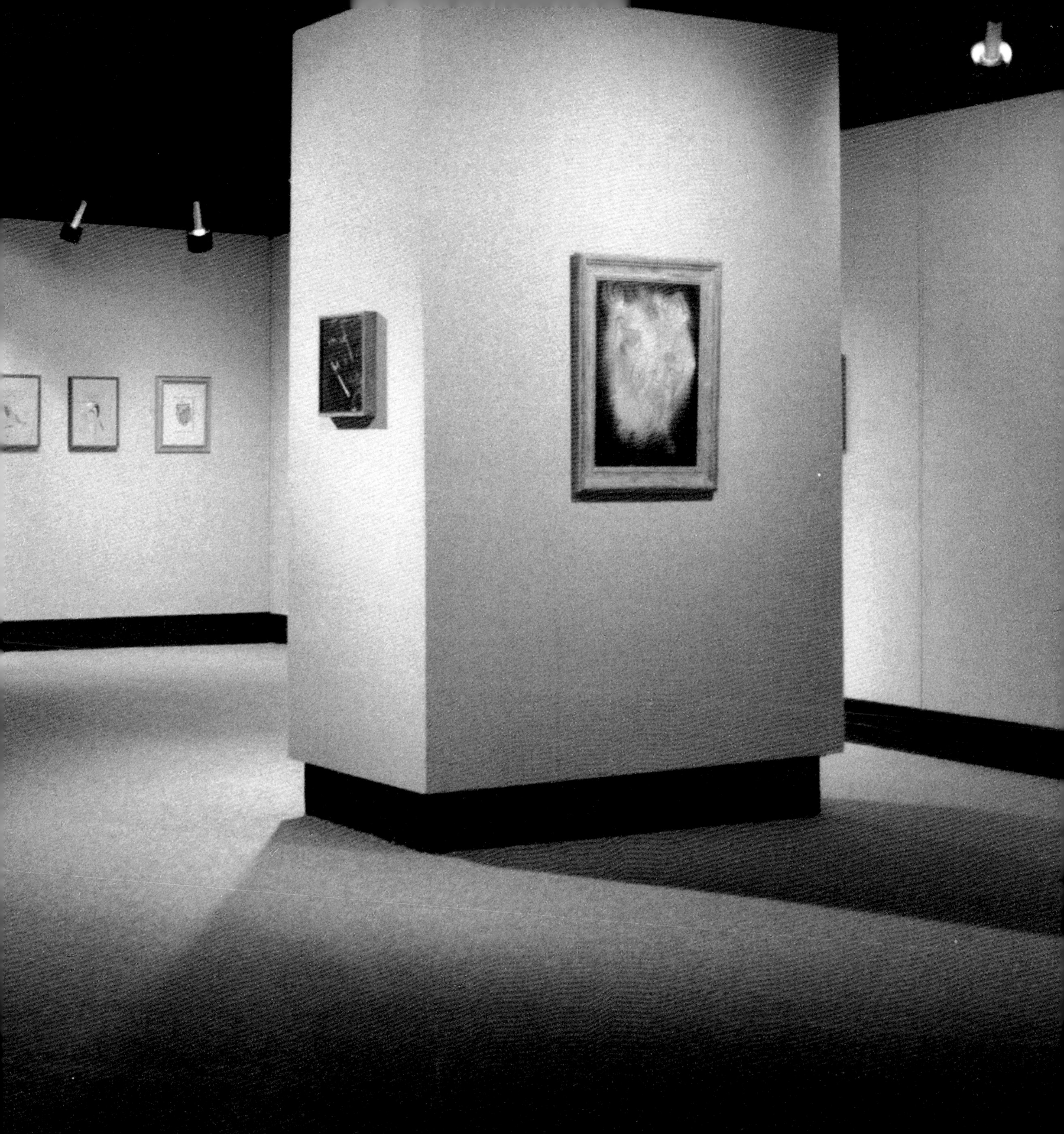

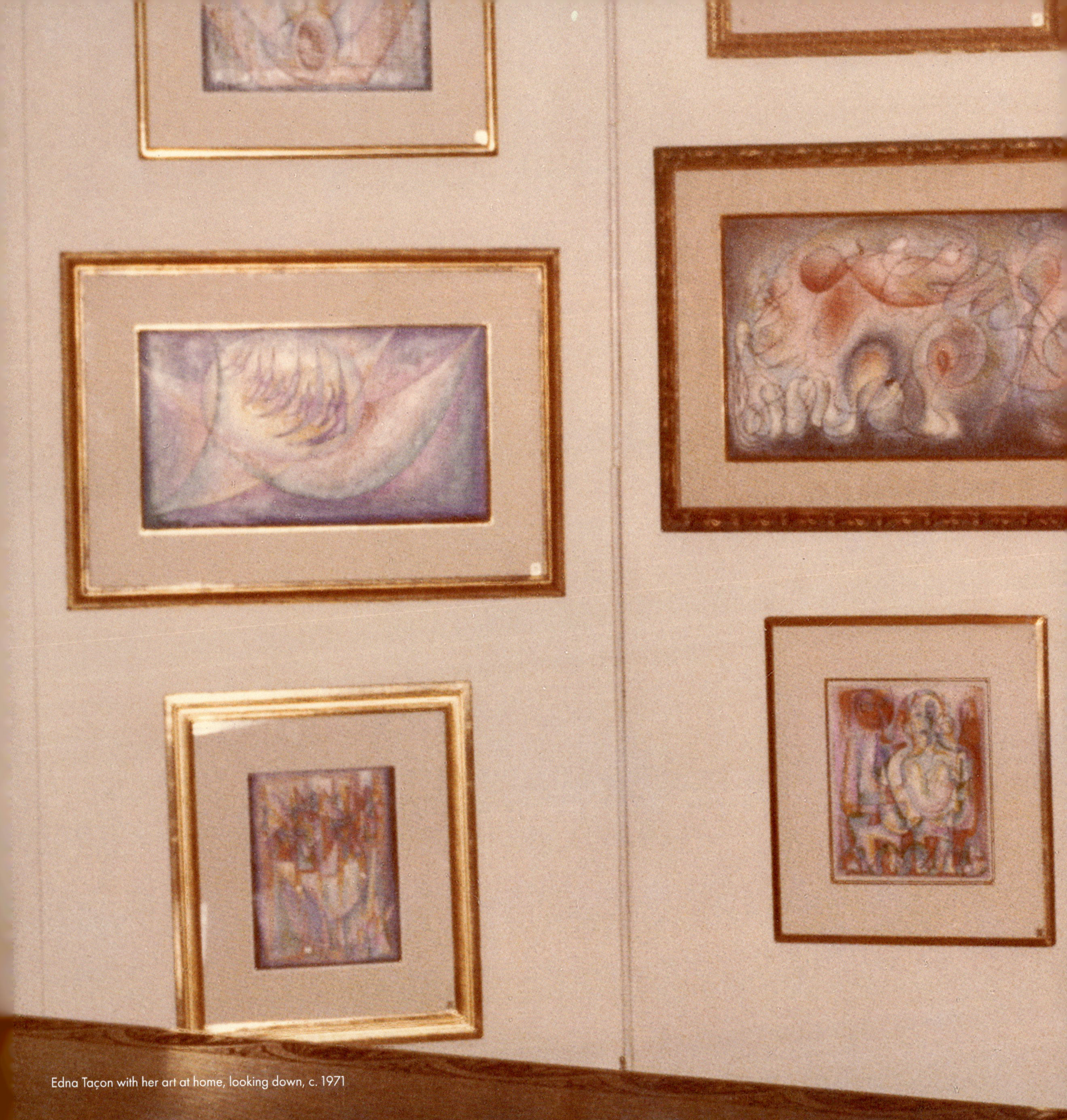

Edna Taçon with her art at home, looking down, c. 1971

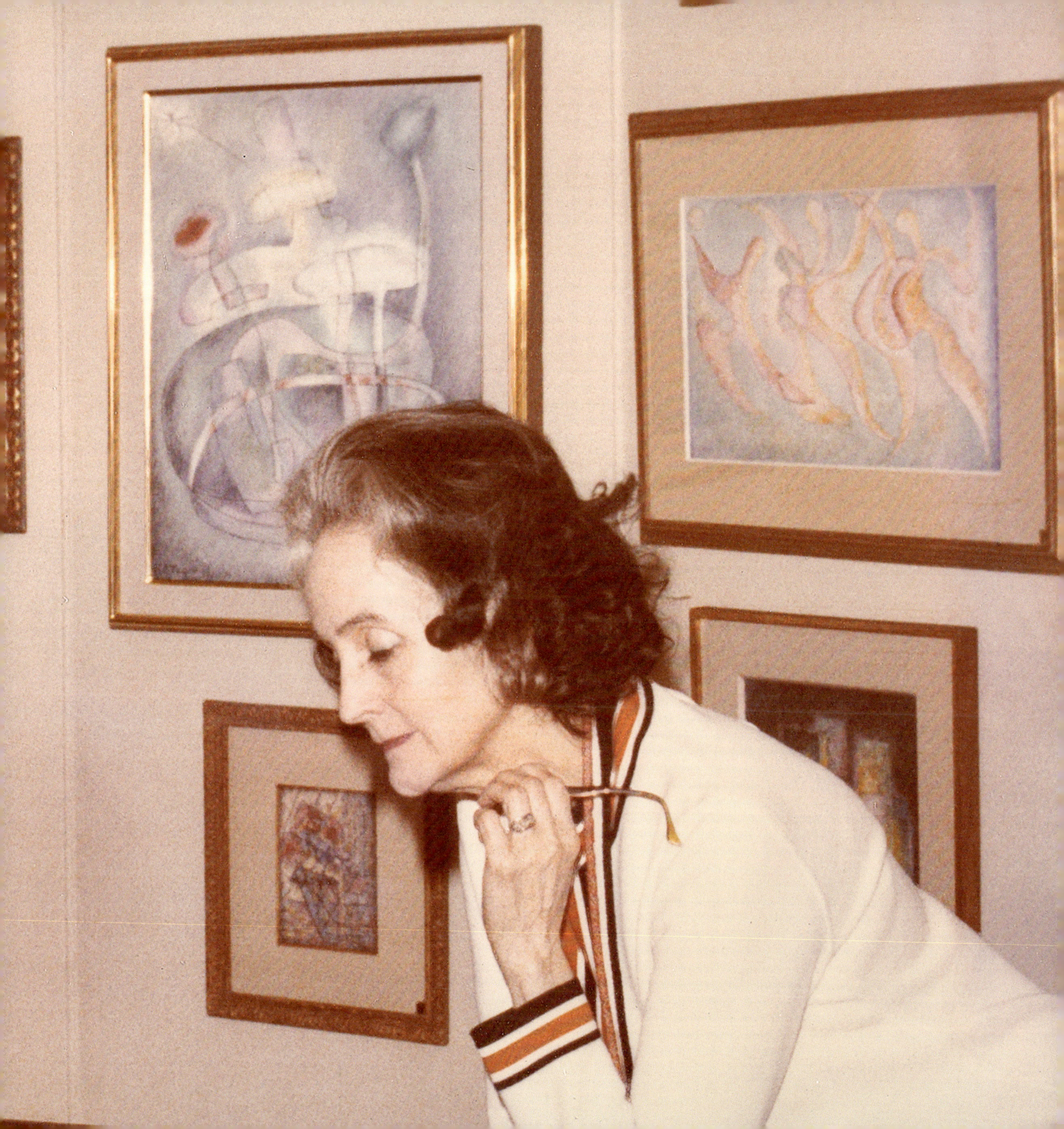

Works Exhibited

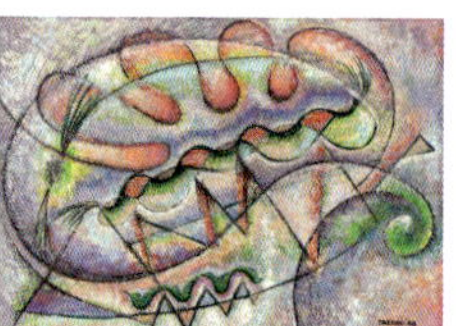

"ABSTRACT"
1948
pen and ink and watercolour on paper
32.9 × 46.7 cm
Art Gallery of Ontario, purchase, with funds from
Joyce and Fred Zemans, 2024
2024/114
pages 60–61

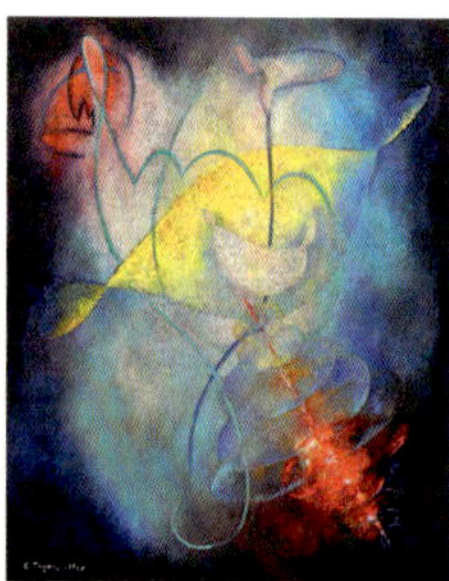

"AURORA"
1945
oil on canvas
106 × 86 cm
Collection of Paul and Susan Taçon
page 88

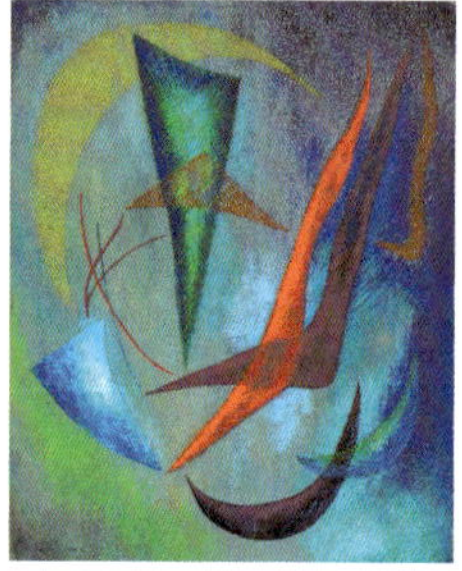

"BLUE NOCTURNE"
1943
watercolour on paper on board
66 × 53.3 cm
Art Gallery of Hamilton, gift of Eva Oram,
2019, former student of Professor Percy Taçon,
College of Education, University of Toronto,
1966
Photo: Mike Lalich, 2025
page 24

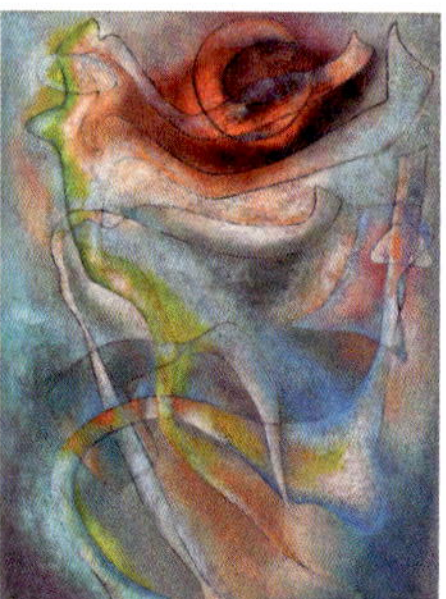

"CAPRICE"
c. 1946
oil on canvas
60.2 × 46 cm
Art Gallery of Ontario, promised gift of
Paul and Susan Taçon
page 54

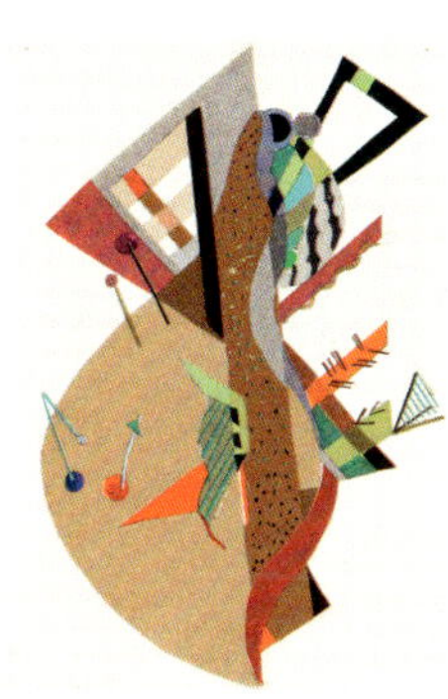

"COMPOSITION"
1940
collage on paper
22.2 × 15.2 cm
Art Gallery of Hamilton, gift of Eva Oram, 2019,
former student of Professor Percy Taçon, College
of Education University of Toronto, 1966
Photo: Mike Lalich, 2025
page 30

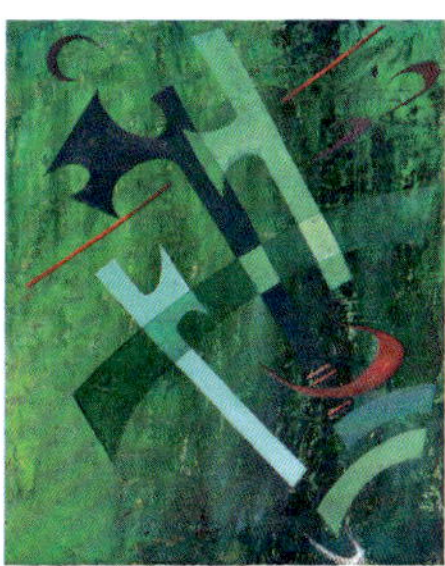

"GREEN ORGANIZATION"
1943
oil on board
30.3 × 24.3 cm
Collection of Paul and Susan Taçon
page 36

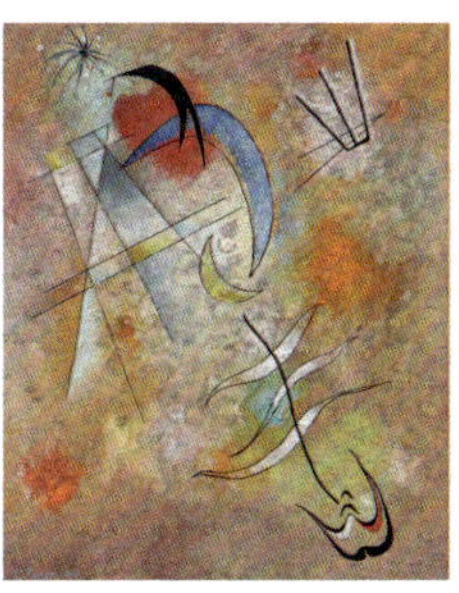

"ECSTASY (BLACK ACCENT)"
1944
oil on canvas
43 × 35.3 cm
Collection of Paul and Susan Taçon
page 55

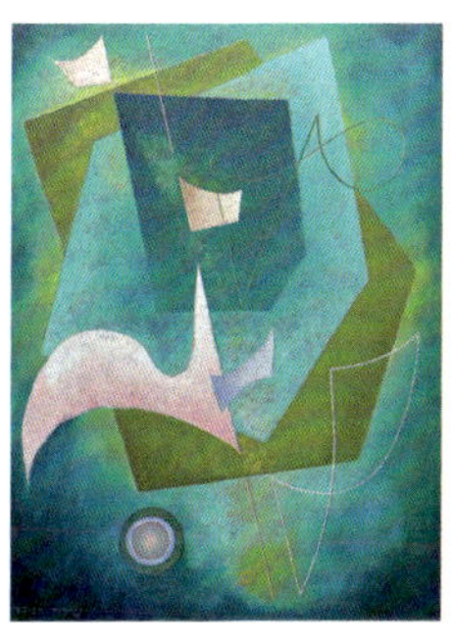

"GREEN SYMPHONY"
1945
oil on canvas
101.6 × 76.8 cm
Private collection, Mississauga
page 49

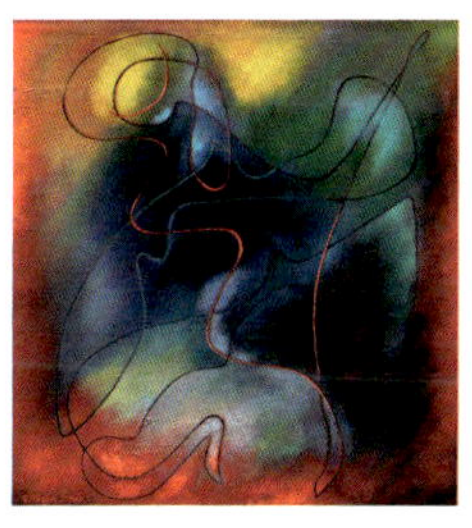

"FLEEING"
1946
oil on canvas board
48.2 × 45.3 cm
Gift of Alexandra Luke, 1967;
Collection of the Robert McLaughlin Gallery,
Oshawa, Ontario
Photo: Laura Findlay
page 63

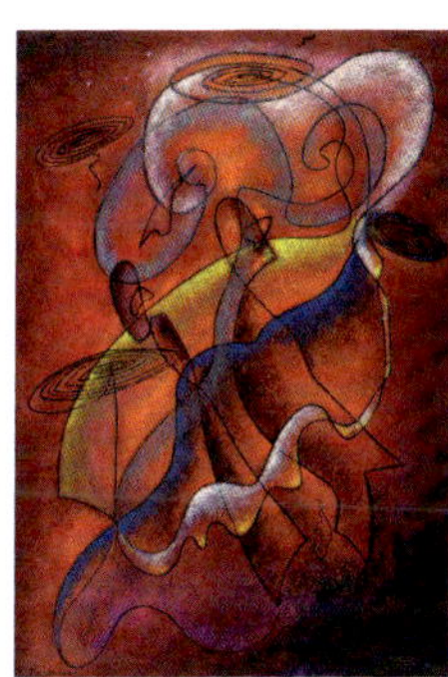

"IMPROVISATION NO. 2"
1946
watercolour and ink on paper
38.8 × 27.6 cm
Art Gallery of Ontario, purchase, 1947
2879
page 25

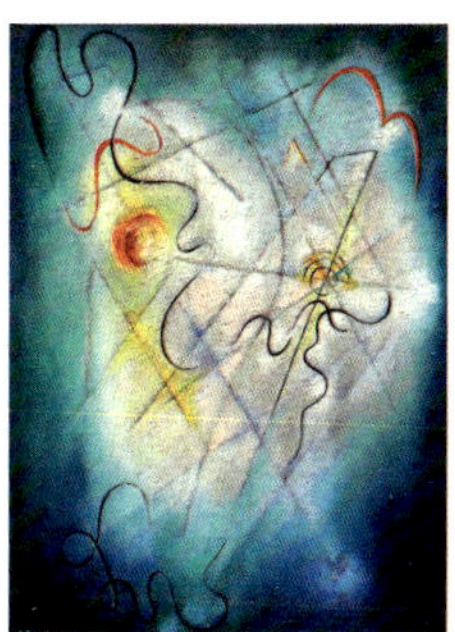

"GAIETY"
1946
oil on canvas board
60.5 × 45.5 cm
Art Gallery of Ontario, purchase, with
funds from Joyce and Fred Zemans, 2019
2019/2266
page 59

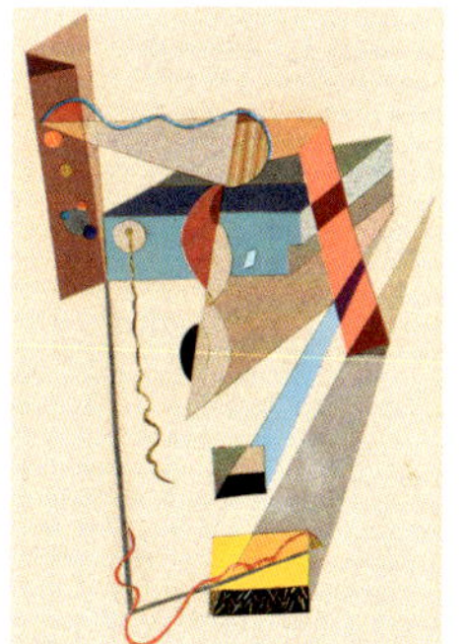

"INVENTION"
c.1941
collage on paper
21.6 × 14.3 cm
Collection of Paul and Susan Taçon
page 33

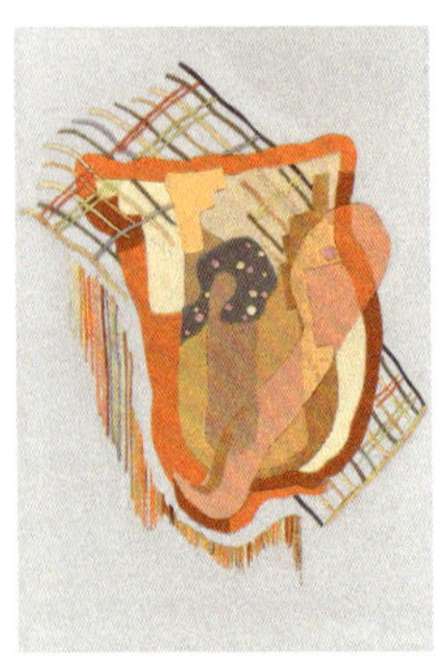

"MAGIC CARPET"
c.1941
collage on paper
22.3 × 14.7 cm
Collection of Paul and Susan Taçon
page 29

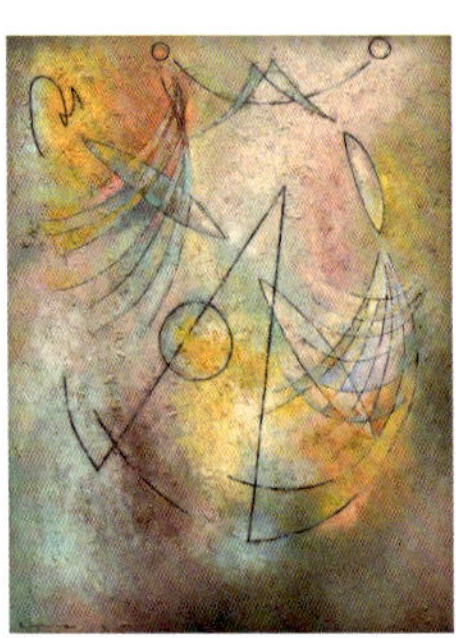

"SWINGING"
1945
oil on canvas board
57.5 × 44.1 cm
Solomon R. Guggenheim Museum, gift,
the artist's estate and Paul Taçon, 2025
2025.27
page 51

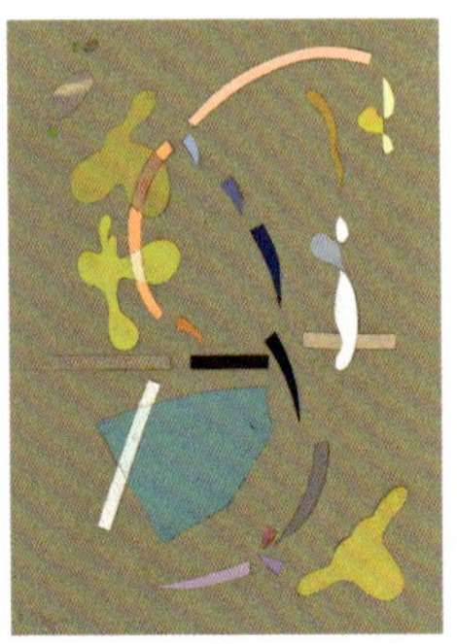

"PRIMAVERA"
c.1940
collage on paper
22.3 × 15.3 cm
Art Gallery of Ontario, promised gift of
Paul and Susan Taçon
page 28

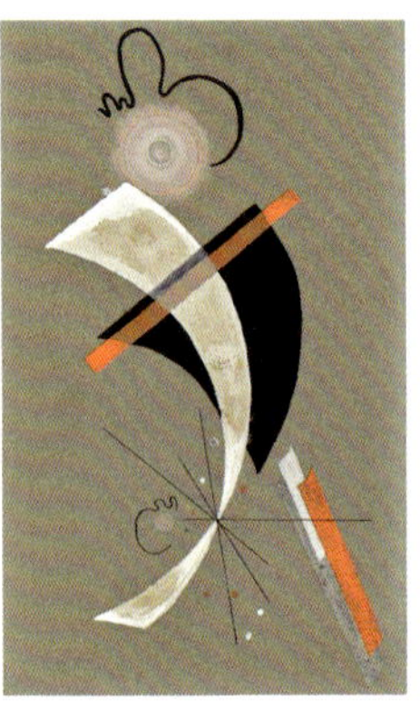

"UNTITLED"
c.1941
pen, ink and gouache on paper
25 × 15.2 cm
Art Gallery of Ontario, promised gift of
Paul and Susan Taçon
page 23

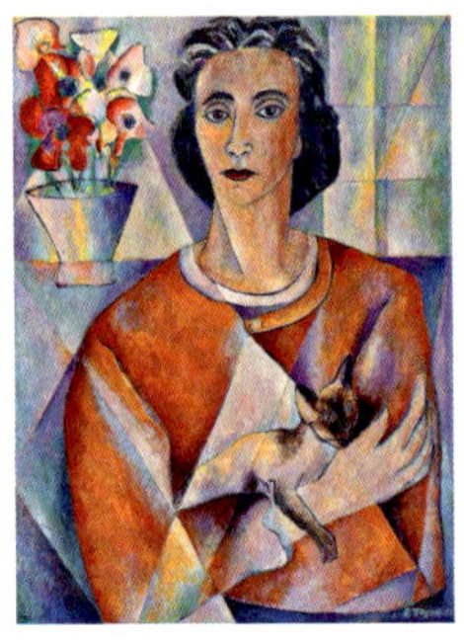

"SELF-PORTRAIT"
1955
opaque watercolour on paper
59.4 × 44.6 cm
Collection of Paul and Susan Taçon
page 67

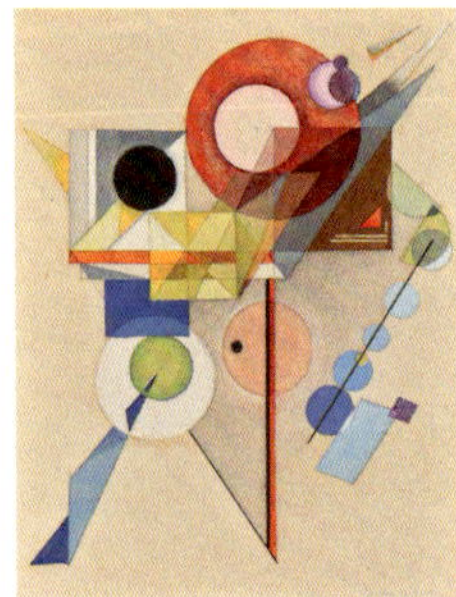

"UNTITLED"
1941
pen and ink with gouache, watercolour,
and graphite on paper
28 × 21.5 cm
Art Gallery of Ontario, promised gift of
Paul and Susan Taçon
page 19

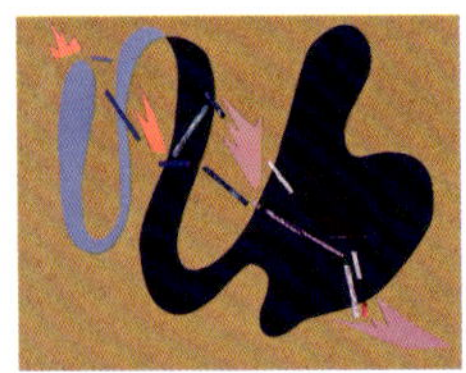

"STUDY IN MOTION"
c.1941
collage on paper
21.5 × 27.9 cm
Collection of Paul and Susan Taçon
page 34

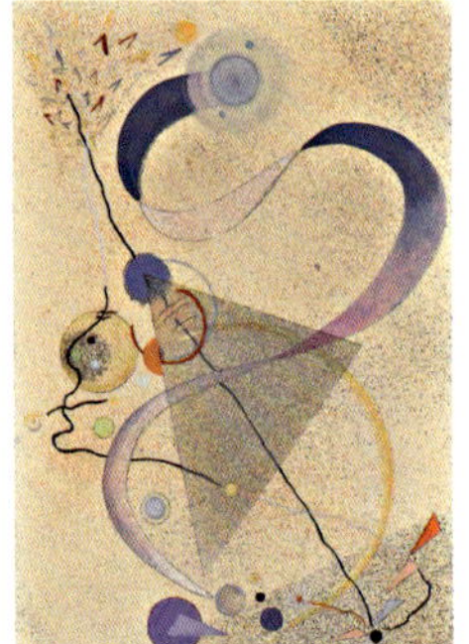

"UNTITLED"
c.1941
pen, ink and watercolour with graphite on
paper
24.9 × 16.8 cm
Art Gallery of Ontario, promised gift of
Paul and Susan Taçon
page 21

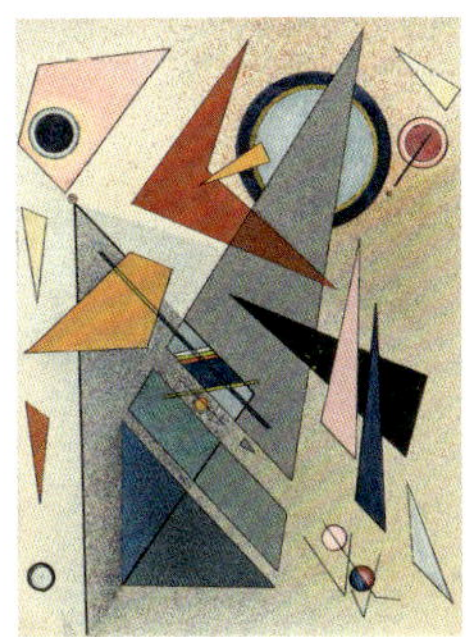

"UNTITLED"
c. 1941
gouache on paper
28 × 22 cm
Collection of Susan Krever and William
Kaplan
page 26

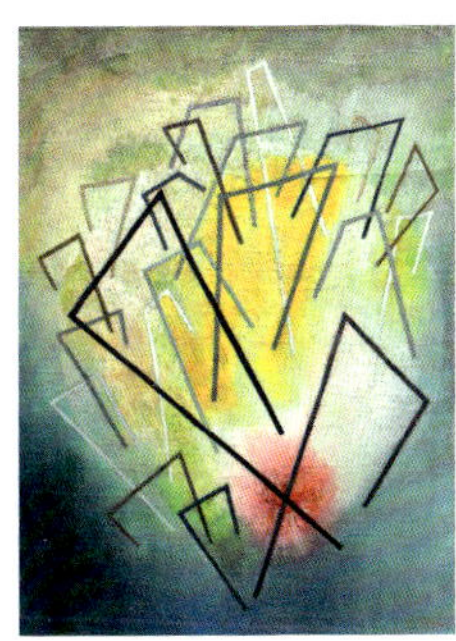

"UNTITLED ABSTRACTION"
1945
oil on canvas
101.6 × 76.2 cm
Collection of Susan Krever and
William Kaplan
page 37

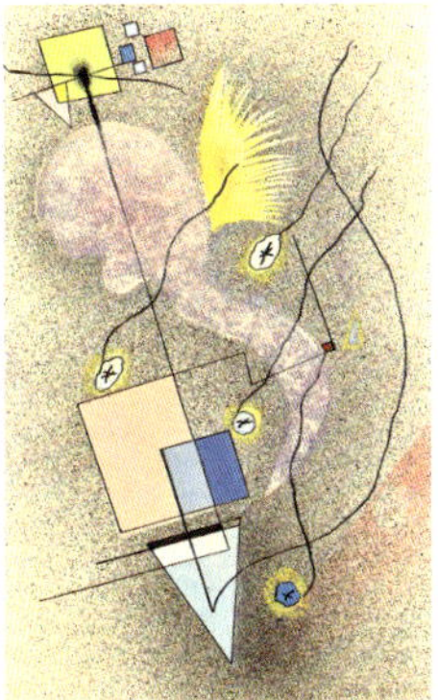

"UNTITLED"
1941
pen and ink with gouache and watercolour on
paper
26.3 × 16.4 cm
Art Gallery of Ontario, promised gift of Paul and
Susan Taçon
page 20

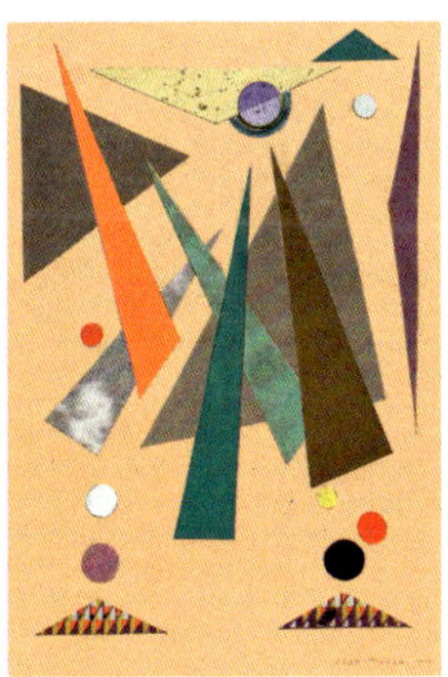

"UNTITLED"
1941
coloured, flocked, and printed paper collage,
mounted to paperboard
29.8 × 19.7 cm
Solomon R. Guggenheim Museum, gift, the artist's
estate and Paul Taçon, 2025
2025.28
page 35

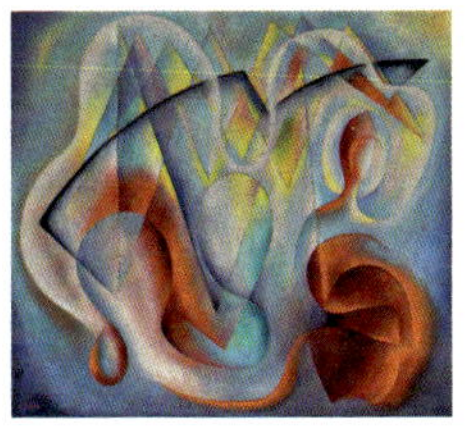

"UNTITLED"
1946–1947
oil on canvas
91 × 105.5 cm
Collection of Paul and Susan Taçon
page 62

Additional Illustrations & Archival Materials

Bertram Brooker
"Chorale" (Bach)
c. 1927
oil on canvas
61 × 43.7 cm
Art Gallery of Ontario, purchase, 1987
87/175
page 22

Wassily Kandinsky
Composition 8 (Komposition 8)
1923
oil on canvas
140 × 201 cm
Solomon R. Guggenheim Museum, New York,
Solomon R. Guggenheim Founding Collection, by gift
37.262
page 18

Marian Dale Scott
Variations on a Theme – Cell and Fossil
1946
oil on board
50 × 60 cm
T. Eaton Company Records, F-229-308-0-1952,
Archives of Ontario
Photo: Commercial Studio at T. Eaton Co.,
Toronto, Canada
page 46

Carl Taçon
Shift
2008
Vermont Mountain White marble
132.08 × 4145.28 × 45.72 cm
Public art commission for One St. Thomas Residences
Photo: Peter Legris
pages 84–85

Carl Taçon and Lyn Carter
Grace Note
2024
painted, roll-formed carbon steel
576.58 × 185.42 × 28.45 cm
Public art commission for MacLaren Art Centre
Photo: Peter Legris
page 83

Edna Taçon
Caricature of Caesar George Finn
January 14, 1929
diary (page 19)
Collection of Paul and Susan Taçon
page 17

Composition
1942
oil on parchment
48.3 × 53.3 cm
Solomon R. Guggenheim Museum, New York,
Solomon R. Guggenheim Founding Collection, by bequest
49.910
page 48

Composition on Pink
1942
oil on parchment
50.8 × 55.9 cm
Solomon R. Guggenheim Museum, New York,
Solomon R. Guggenheim Founding Collection, by bequest
49.949
page 50

Egg sketch
1967
drawing
20 × 13 cm
Edna Taçon fonds, Edward P. Taylor Library & Archives,
Art Gallery of Ontario, promised gift of
Paul and Susan Taçon
Box 3
page 74

Evolving (black-and-white documentation)
1946
watercolour
artwork dimensions unknown (photo: 25.5 × 21 cm)
T. Eaton Company Records, F-229-308-0-1957,
Archives of Ontario
page 106

◆ *Kites sketch*
1957
drawing
9 × 5 cm
Edna Taçon fonds, Edward P. Taylor Library & Archives, Art
Gallery of Ontario, promised gift of Paul and Susan Taçon
Box 3
page 74

Eaton's ad for *Excursion in Abstract* with drawings
by Fritz Brandtner
January 27, 1945
59 × 19 cm (sheet)
T. Eaton Company Records, F-229-143-0-1,
Archives of Ontario
page 56

Eaton's ad for *Non-Objective Paintings*
January 1944
29.5 × 6.5 cm (full clipping)
T. Eaton Company Records, F-229-143-0-1,
Archives of Ontario
page 42

◆ Eaton's ad for *Twenty Paintings by Edna Taçon*
January 21, 1947
newspaper advertisement
16 × 18 cm
Edna Taçon fonds, Edward P. Taylor Library &
Archives, Art Gallery of Ontario, promised gift
of Paul and Susan Taçon
Box 2, File 4
page 64

Eaton's fall exhibitions announcement in *Canadian
Review of Music and Art*, vol. 3, nos. 7–8
1944
27 × 19 cm (sheet)
T. Eaton Company Records, F-229-143-0-1,
Archives of Ontario
page 43

Edna Arnold's passport
1968
18.5 × 15.5 cm
Edna Taçon fonds, Edward P. Taylor Library &
Archives, Art Gallery of Ontario, promised gift
of Paul and Susan Taçon
Box 2, File 18
page 112

◆ Edna Taçon holding a violin
c. 1920s
photograph
17 × 28 cm
Edna Taçon fonds, Edward P. Taylor Library &
Archives, Art Gallery of Ontario, promised gift
of Paul and Susan Taçon
Box 2, File 10
Photo: Melbourne Photo Studios
page 14

Edna Taçon teaching at the Ontario College of Art
July 23, 1946
photograph
10 × 13 cm
Ontario College of Art and Design Records,
fonds 1266, item 106542, Toronto City Archives
pages 72–73

◆ Edna Taçon wearing a hat
c. 1950s
photograph
34.5 × 28.5 cm
Edna Taçon fonds, Edward P. Taylor Library & Archives,
Art Gallery of Ontario, promised gift of Paul and
Susan Taçon
Box 4
page 6

◆ Edna Taçon with her art at home
c. 1971
photograph
12.5 × 9 cm
Edna Taçon fonds, Edward P. Taylor Library & Archives,
Art Gallery of Ontario, promised gift of Paul and
Susan Taçon
Box 2, File 9
page 76

Edna Taçon with her art at home, looking down
c. 1971
photograph
12.5 × 9 cm
Edna Taçon fonds, Edward P. Taylor Library & Archives,
Art Gallery of Ontario, promised gift of
Paul and Susan Taçon
Box 2, File 9
pages 92–93

"Edna Taçon's Contextualist Art Wins Admiration
at Eaton Gallery," written by Pearl McCarthy in
The Globe and Mail
January 25, 1947
newspaper article
15 × 19 cm
Edna Taçon fonds, Edward P. Taylor Library & Archives,
Art Gallery of Ontario, promised gift of Paul and
Susan Taçon
Box 2, File 4
page 65

◆ Envelope addressed to Edna Taçon
1948
11.4 × 24.13 cm
Edna Taçon fonds, Edward P. Taylor Library & Archives,
Art Gallery of Ontario, promised gift of Paul and
Susan Taçon
Box 2, File 4
*Not illustrated

◆ Exhibition pamphlet for *Edna Taçon: Contextualist*,
Chinese Gallery
1946
10 × 20 cm
Edna Taçon fonds, Edward P. Taylor Library & Archives,
Art Gallery of Ontario, promised gift of
Paul and Susan Taçon
Box 2, File 1
page 64

Exhibition pamphlet for *Edna Taçon: Exhibition
of Paintings*, Nicholas Roerich Museum
1971
15 × 23 cm
Edna Taçon fonds, Edward P. Taylor Library & Archives,
Art Gallery of Ontario, promised gift of Paul and
Susan Taçon
Box 2, File 1
pages 70–71

◆ Exhibition pamphlet for *Edna Taçon: Outstanding
Canadian Non-Objective Painter*,
Eaton's Fine Art Galleries
1945
13.5 × 21.5cm
Edna Taçon Artist File
Edward P. Taylor Library & Archives,
Art Gallery of Ontario
page 57

Exhibition pamphlet for *Edna Taçon:
Exponent of Non-Objective Painting*,
Eaton's Fine Art Galleries
1944
Edward P. Taylor Library & Archives,
Art Gallery of Ontario
Box 1
pages 44–45

◆ Exhibition pamphlet for *Non-Objective Pictures
(Paintings and Paper Plastics)* by Edna Taçon,
Studio 83, New York City
1941
15.5 × 11.5 cm
Edna Taçon Artist File
Edward P. Taylor Library & Archives, Art Gallery
of Ontario
pages 8–9

◆ Exhibition pamphlet for *Taçon*, Chinese Gallery
c. 1946
21 × 15 cm
Edna Taçon fonds, Edward P. Taylor Library & Archives,
Art Gallery of Ontario, promised gift of Paul and
Susan Taçon
Box 2, File 1
page 64

◆ Home interior
c. 1971
photograph
9 × 12.5 cm
Edna Taçon fonds, Edward P. Taylor Library & Archives,
Art Gallery of Ontario, promised gift of Paul and Susan
Taçon
Box 2, File 9
page 78

*Kathleen Munn and Edna Taçon:
New Perspectives on Modernism in Canada*
(installation view), Art Gallery of York University
1988
photograph
10 × 15.5 cm
Edna Taçon fonds, Edward P. Taylor Library & Archives,
Art Gallery of Ontario, promised gift of Paul and
Susan Taçon
Box 2, File 16
pages 90–91

Letter from Carl Taçon to Joyce Zemans
September 13, 1986
27.9 × 21.6 cm
York University Libraries, Clara Thomas Archives &
Special Collections, Joyce Zemans fonds, F0765
page 82

Letter from Marcel Marceau
c. 1960
ink on paper
21.5 × 16.5 cm
Art Gallery of Ontario, Edward P. Taylor Library
& Archives
Box 2, File 20
page 81

Photograph of painting of Marcel Marceau
by Edna Taçon
1958
11.5 × 9 cm
Edna Taçon fonds, Edward P. Taylor Library &
Archives, Art Gallery of Ontario, promised gift of
Paul and Susan Taçon
Box 2, File 20
page 80

Photograph of portrait of Marcel Marceau by
Edna Taçon, autographed by Marceau
c. 1960
9 × 9 cm
Edna Taçon fonds, Edward P. Taylor Library &
Archives, Art Gallery of Ontario, promised gift of
Paul and Susan Taçon
Box 2, File 20
page 80

Portrait of Edna Taçon
c. 1946
photograph
20.5 × 25 cm
T. Eaton Company Records, F-229-308-0-1957,
Archives of Ontario
Photo: Charmante Studio, Inc. New York
facing page 1

Restaurant mural by Edna Taçon
c. 1940s
3 gelatin silver prints
25.5 × 20 cm (each)
Edna Taçon fonds, Edward P. Taylor Library &
Archives, Art Gallery of Ontario, promised gift
of Paul and Susan Taçon
Box 2, File 15
* *The two photographs with figures are exhibited.*
pages 40–41

◆ Scrapbook set to page with installation image of
Edna Taçon's works at Museum of Non-Objective
Painting
c. 1940s
48 × 30 cm (open)
Edna Taçon fonds, Edward P. Taylor Library &
Archives, Art Gallery of Ontario, promised gift
of Paul and Susan Taçon
Box 1
* Not illustrated

Scrapbook set to page with image of
Composition on Pink
c. 1940s
48 × 30 cm (open)
Edna Taçon fonds, Edward P. Taylor Library &
Archives, Art Gallery of Ontario, promised gift of
Paul and Susan Taçon
Box 1
pages 108–9

Scrapbook set to page with image of Eaton's ad
for the fourth annual exhibition of non-objective art
by Edna Taçon
c. 1940s
48 × 30 cm (open)
Edna Taçon fonds, Edward P. Taylor Library &
Archives, Art Gallery of Ontario, promised gift of
Paul and Susan Taçon
Box 1
pages 110–11

◆ "Some Husbands Pick Wives' Hats, Others Just
Pay and Ignore 'Em," written by Dorothy Howarth in
The Evening Telegram
July 25, 1946
newspaper article
30 × 16 cm (sheet)
Edna Taçon fonds, Edward P. Taylor Library &
Archives, Art Gallery of Ontario, promised gift of
Paul and Susan Taçon
Box 2, File 6
page 86

Third solo exhibition at Eaton's (installation view)
January 1944
photograph
22 × 25 cm
Edna Taçon fonds, Edward P. Taylor Library &
Archives, Art Gallery of Ontario, promised gift of
Paul and Susan Taçon
Box 1
pages 52–53

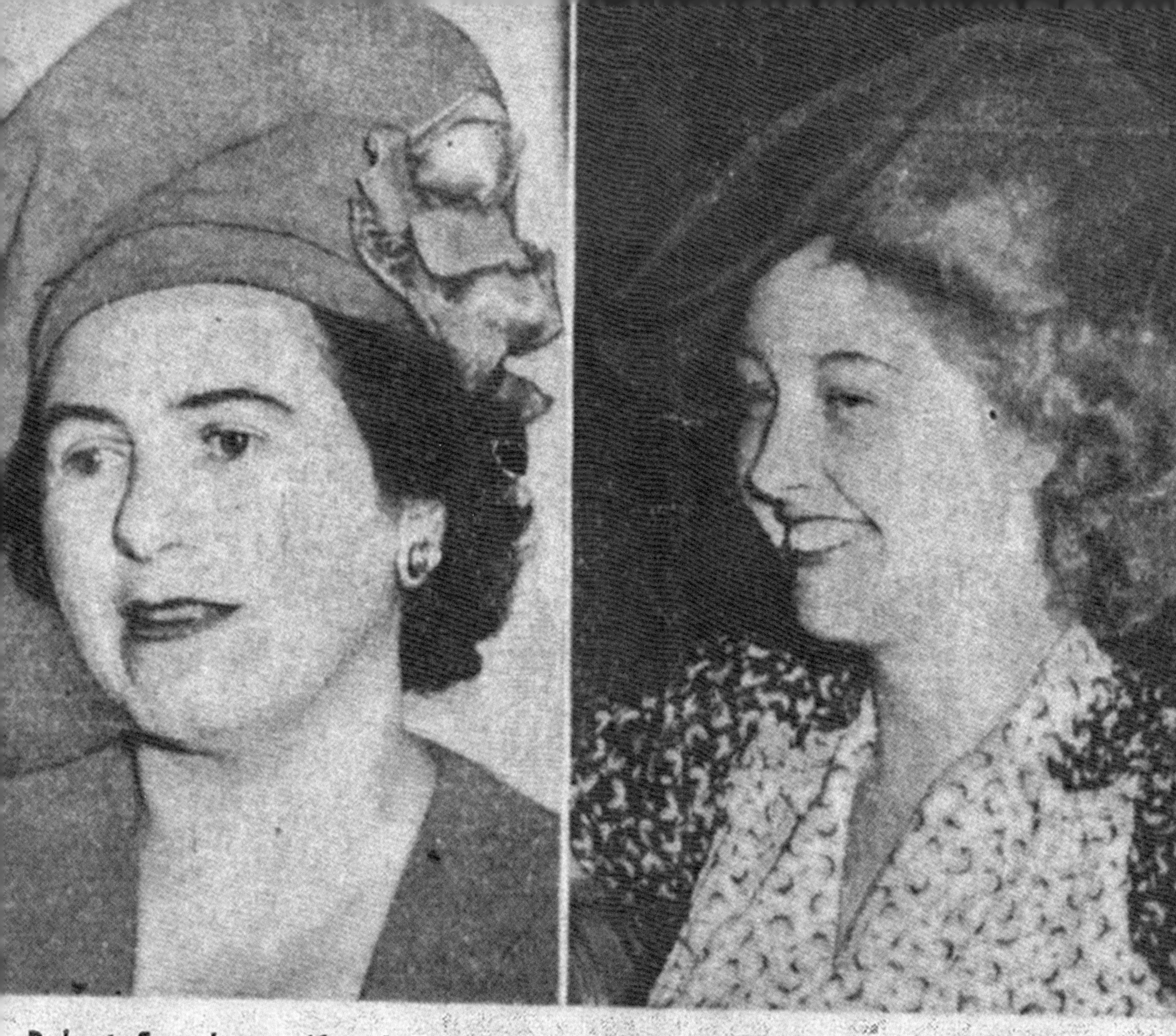

Robert Saunders, wife of To-
o's Mayor, wears a turquoise blue
her husband likes. Much like the
en's favorite style, it increases
Saunders' resemblance to Her
Majesty.

This hat is the men's favorite color,
red, and Fred Jones (Mr. Average
Toronto) likes his wife in it better
than any other. She lost it once, and
he was much upset until it turned up
safely.

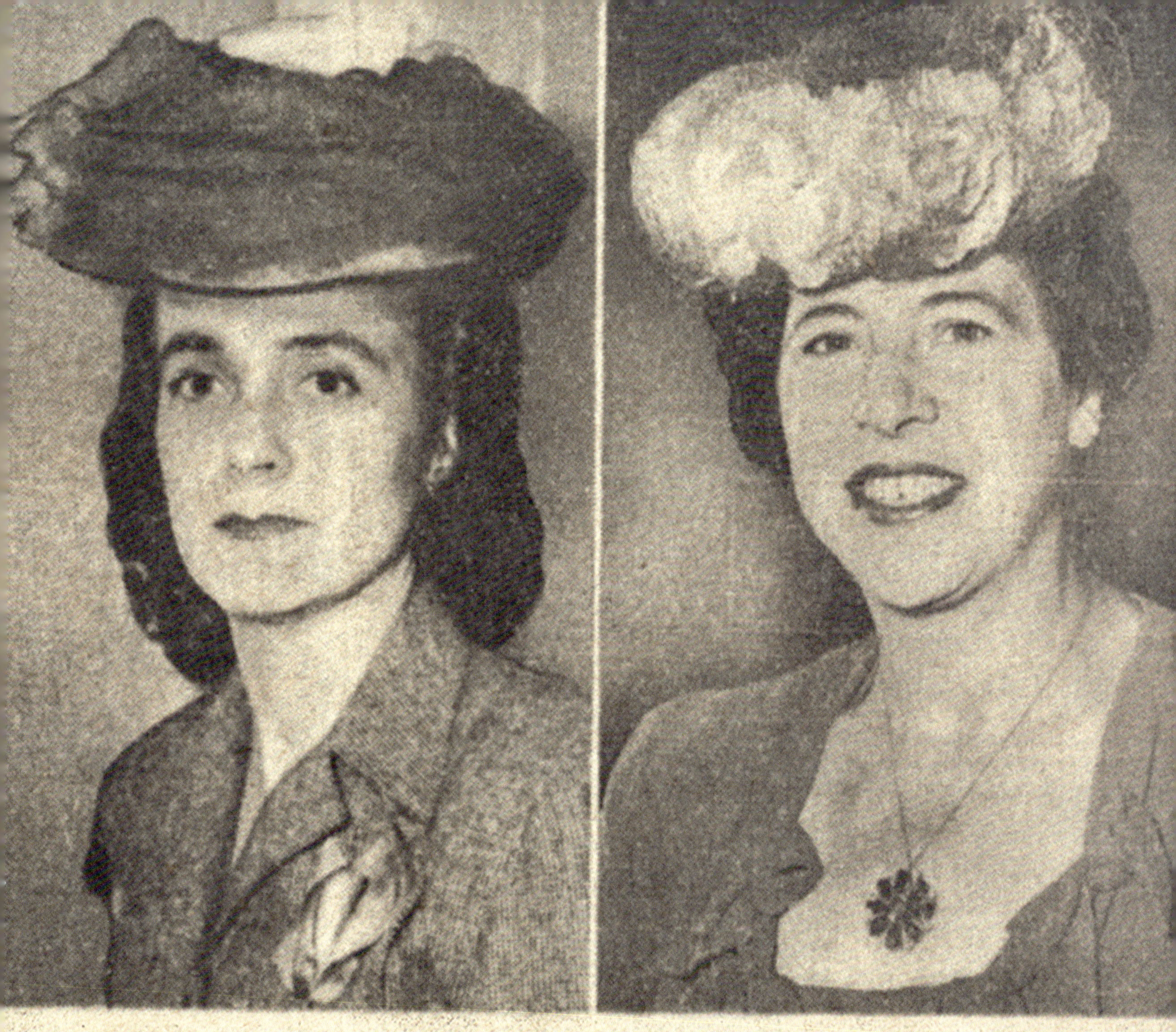

Edna Tacon, non-objective painter, designs her own hats, and her husband really likes them. This one is ice-white straw with touch of black velvet ribbon, surrounded by flame-colored tulle.

Mrs. Fred Hawes, wife of "Frederic", one of Canada's better known hat designers, is sure her husband likes her hats, for he creates them. She wears a circle of shell-pink roses covered with bronze veil.

Editor:
Renée van der Avoird

Managing Editor:
Jim Shedden

Publishing Coordinator:
Robyn Lew

Production and Content Editor:
Nives Hajdin-Rorabeck

Designer:
Alina Skyson

Research Assistants:
Emily Coneybeare
Patricia Ritacca
Kimberley Rush-Duyguluer

Curatorial Coordinator:
Tammy Law

Proofreader:
David Marsh

Photographer:
Craig Boyko

Pre-Press:
Paul Jerinkitsch

Printing:
Friesens

Printed and bound in Canada.
Printed on 100 lb. Matte FSC White (text)
and Rainbow Antique FSC (cover).
Set in Futura PT by Paratype and Rillus
by Formagari.

ISBN: 9781773104553

10 9 8 7 6 5 4 3 2 1

Library and Archives Canada Cataloguing in Publication

Title: Edna Taçon / edited by Renée van der Avoird.
Names: van der Avoird, Renée, editor. | Art Gallery of Ontario, host institution, publisher.
Description: Catalogue of an exhibition held at the Art Gallery of Ontario. | Includes bibliographical references.
Identifiers: Canadiana 20250180340 | ISBN 9781773104553 (hardcover)
Subjects: LCSH: Taçon, Edna, 1905-1980—Exhibitions. | LCGFT: Exhibition catalogs.
Classification: LCC ND249.T25 A4 2026 | DDC 759.11—dc23

Art Gallery of Ontario
317 Dundas Street West
Toronto, Ontario M5T 1G4
Canada
ago.ca

The Art Gallery of Ontario is partially funded by the Ontario Ministry of Culture. Additional operating support is received from the City of Toronto, the Department of Canadian Heritage, and the Canada Council for the Arts.

Contemporary programming at the Art Gallery of Ontario is supported by

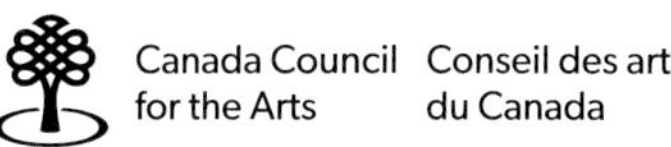

The AGO would like to acknowledge the support of the Richard and Beryl Ivey Canadian Art Fund for the Edna Taçon Study Days.

Goose Lane Editions
500 Beaverbrook Court, Suite 330
Fredericton, New Brunswick E3B 5X4
Canada
gooselane.com

Goose Lane Editions is located on the unceded territory of the Wəlastəkwiyik whose ancestors along with the Mi'kmaq and Peskotomuhkati Nations signed Peace and Friendship Treaties with the British Crown in the 1700s.

Goose Lane Editions acknowledges the generous support of the Government of Canada, the Canada Council for the Arts, and the Government of New Brunswick.

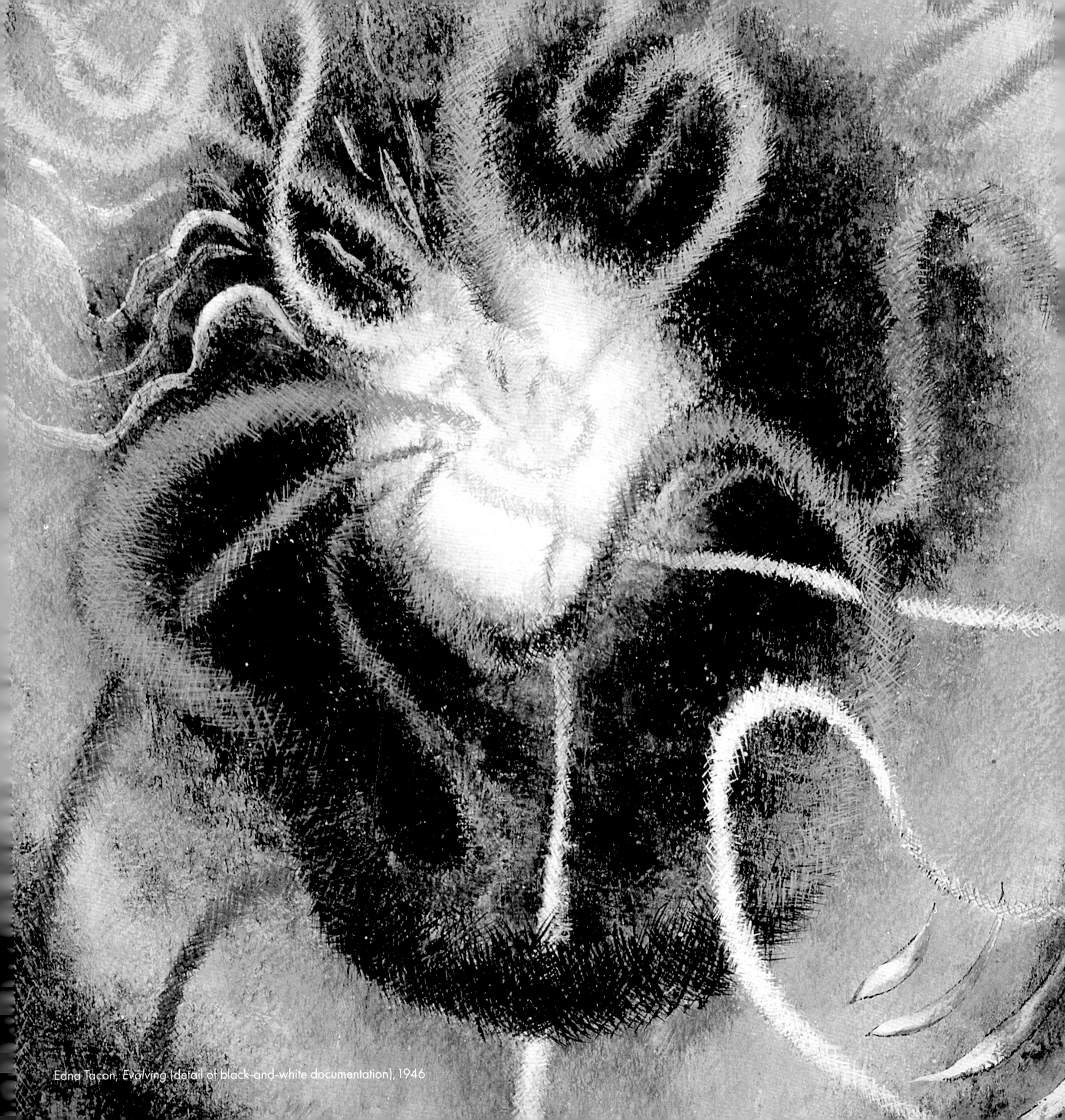

Edna Tacon, Evolving (detail of black-and-white documentation), 1946

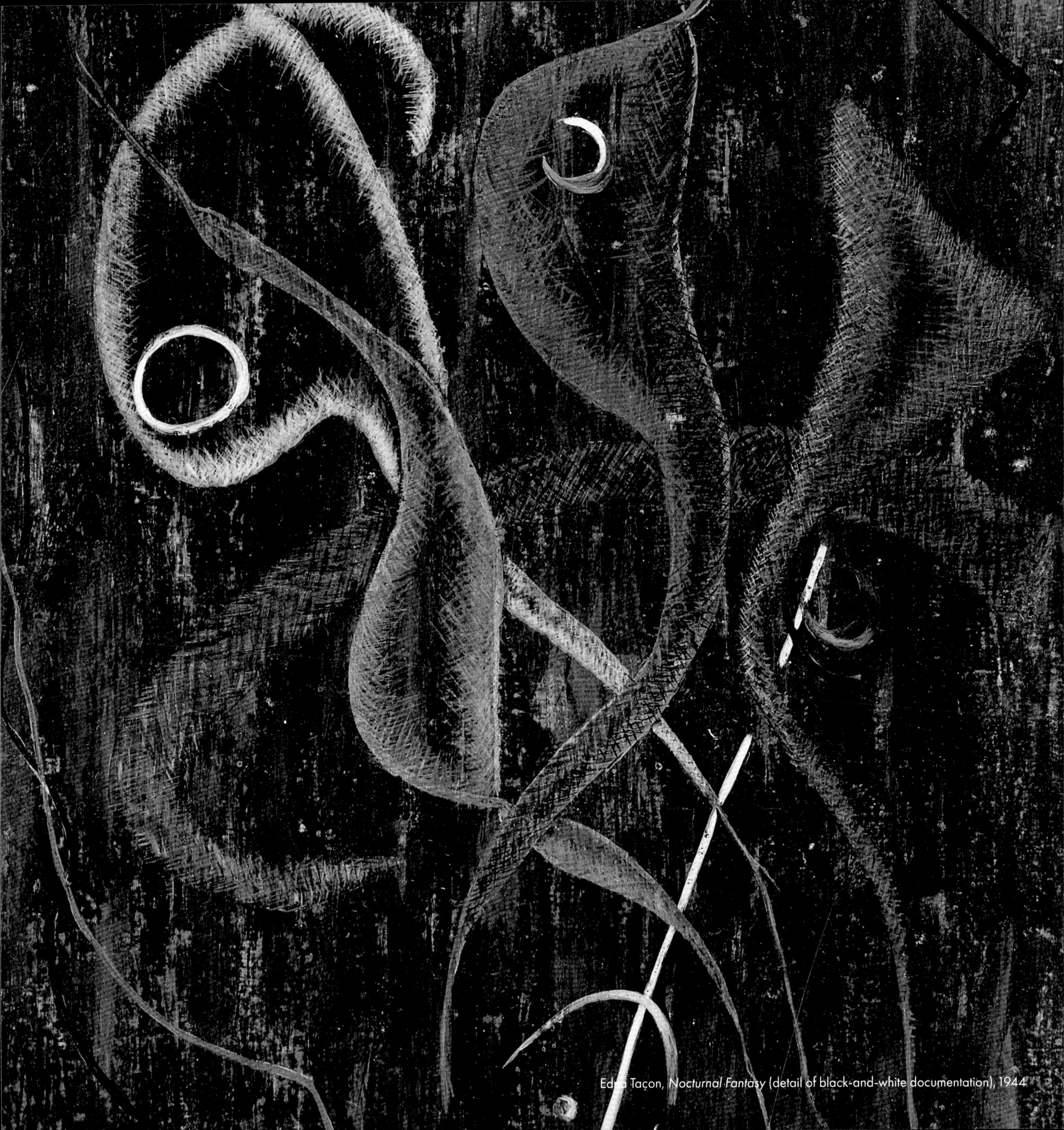

Edna Taçon, *Nocturnal Fantasy* (detail of black-and-white documentation), 1944

"Composition on Pink" - 1943.
Loan Exhibition April 15th, 1944.
Museum of Non-objective Painting
24 East 54th Street. New York. N.Y.

Purchased by Solomon R. Guggenheim -

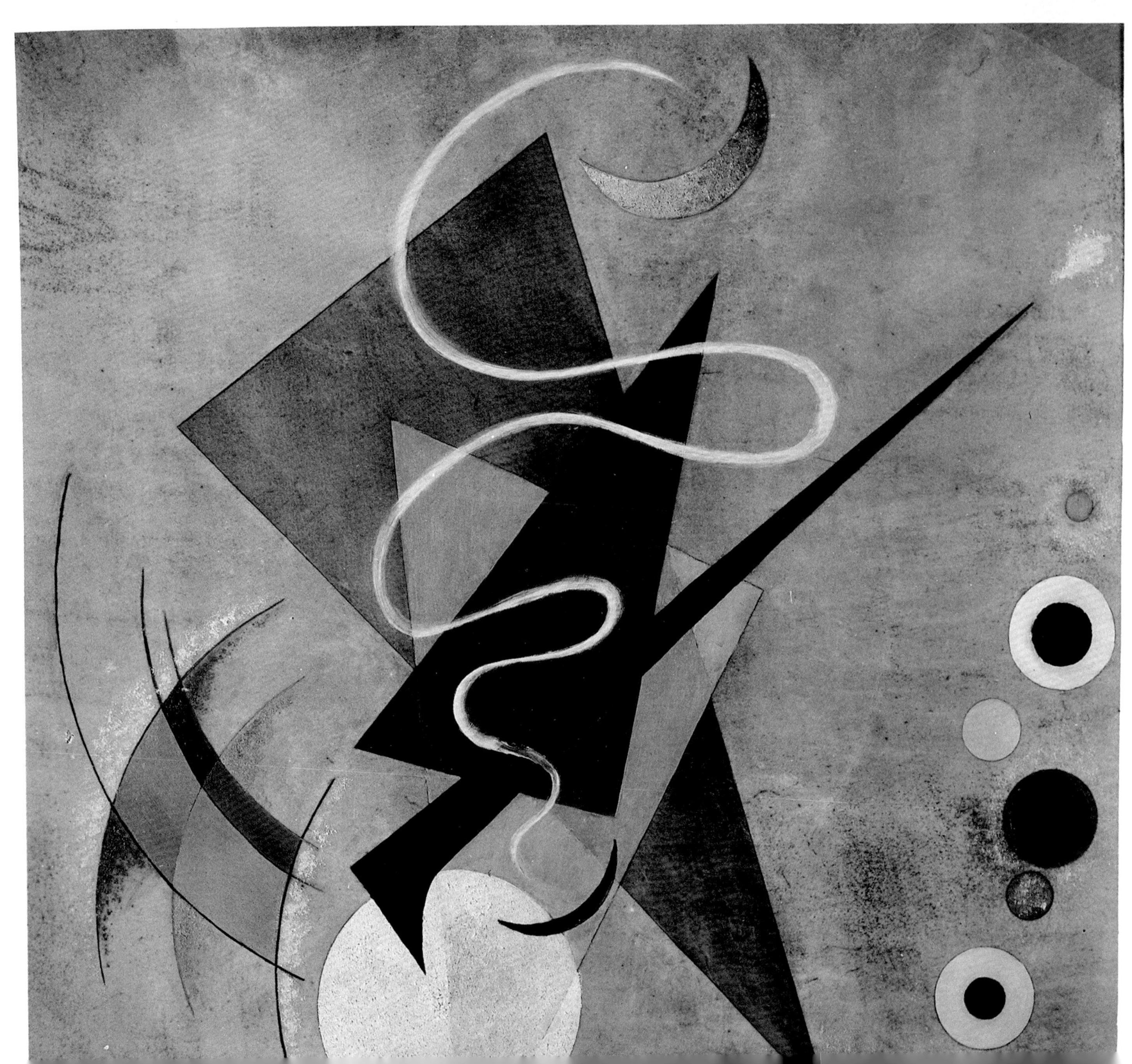

EDNA TAÇON

EXPONENT ON NON-OBJECTIVE PAINTING

Edna Taçon holds an increasing place in the international field of non-objective art. It was after achieving success as a musician that she was captured by the rhythm and form of visual art. Painting also offered her, as a tool of expression, the use of colour, in which she is particularly gifted; and, as representative painting did not satisfy her æsthetic needs, she naturally turned to the intuitive creation of non-objective art. Her husband, a painter and instructor, fostered this interest.

Scholarships from the Solomon Guggenheim Foundation of New York recognized a new talent in the field, and, by assiduous work, Mrs. Taçon has met demands for numerous exhibitions in the United States and Canada. She became a member of the staff of the Guggenheim Foundation in 1943.

Born in the United States of Scottish and French ancestry but brought up in Canada, Mrs. Taçon studied violin in Europe and America with Geza de Kresz, Louis Persinger, William Primrose, Oscar Studer.

Globe Mail   Sept 25, 1948

EATON'S · COLLEGE STREET

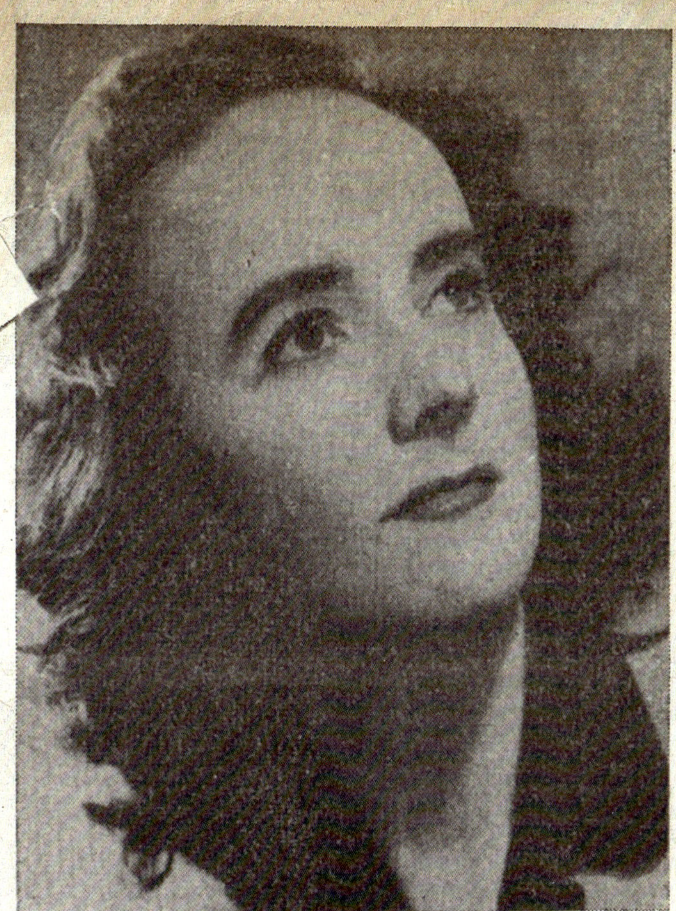

Miss Tacon, a member of the Solomon R. Guggenheim Foundation, will be in the Gallery during her Exhibition, and will be glad to answer any questions.

Announcing the Fourth
Annual Exhibition of

NON-OBJECTIVE ART

by Edna Tacon

Once more we welcome to the Fine Art Galleries this gifted young Hamilton artist, who, like so many creative artists, finds in non-objective art the highest

MUSEUM OF NON-OBJECTIVE PAINTING

NEW LOAN EXHIBITION

ANDERSON	KLEIN
AUTORINO	LASSAW
ASH	MASON
BERTOIA	MATTERN
BIEL	MOHOLY-NAGY
BRILLINGER	PHELPS
DREWES	REBAY
FINE	REICHMAN-LEWIS
FISCHINGER	RUSSELL
HOHENBERG	SCARLETT
JOHNSON	SENNHAUSER
KAMROWSKI	STAPP
KERN	TACON
KERNS	XCERON

SOLOMON R. GUGGENHEIM FOUNDATION

24 East 54th Street, New York City
OPEN Sundays 12-6 — weekdays 10-6

NEW YORK SUNDAY TIMES. JANUARY 16
1944.

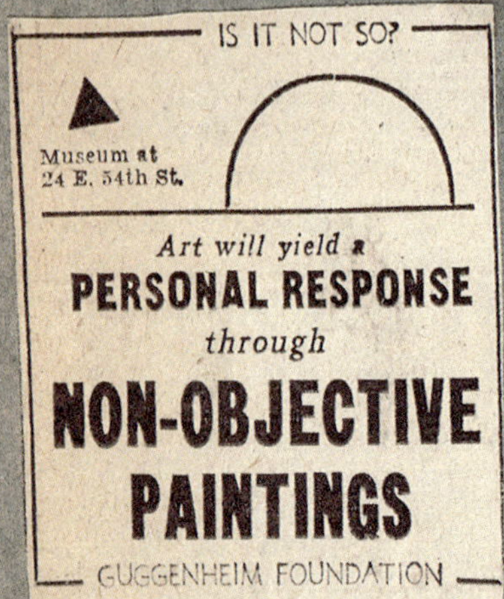